She Went A-Whaling

THE JOURNAL OF MARTHA SMITH BREWER BROWN

She Went A-Whaling

THE JOURNAL OF
MARTHA SMITH BREWER BROWN
FROM ORIENT, LONG ISLAND, NEW YORK,
AROUND THE WORLD
ON THE WHALING SHIP
Lucy Ann, 1847-1849

TRANSCRIBED AND EDITED BY
ANNE MACKAY

WITH A FOREWORD BY
JOAN DRUETT

AND INTRODUCTION BY
DONALD H. BOERUM

FOR THE
OYSTERPONDS HISTORICAL SOCIETY

Funding for *She Went A-Whaling* has been provided
by several generous gifts.

Special funds have been given in memory of:

JEAN ROY MILLAR
(1930-1991)
fearless in the stormy winds and waves.

JANICE MOUNT SHRUHAN
(1926-1991)
a sailor and woman who loved the sea.

THE OYSTERPONDS HISTORICAL SOCIETY

Founded in 1945, the Oysterponds Historical Society is a not-for-profit corporation with 6 historic buildings and extensive collections of local artifacts, including many which belonged to Martha Brown and her husband, Captain Edwin Brown. Located on Village Lane, Orient, N.Y., it is open to the public several afternoons a week mid-June through September.

President . . . . Fredrica Wachsberger

For more information about OHS collections and exhibits, write to: OHS, P.O. Box 844, Orient, NY 11957

ISBN 0-9631911-2-8

Produced by Ten Percent Publishing
200 West 70th Street
Suite 10-G
New York, NY 10023
Project coordinator: Manuela Soares
Design and typography: Sara Yager

Printed in the United States of America

10 9 8 7 6 5 4 3 2

CONTENTS

ACKNOWLEDGMENTS

We are indebted to the great granddaughters of Martha Brown who preserved her letters and journal—Barbara Prince Hughes and Phyllis Edwards Hale. Martha's granddaughter Mildred Prince collected many of the materials and was the first to transcribe excerpts from the Journal. Constance J. Terry was instrumental in publishing Captain Brown's logs, *In the Wake of Whales*.

Donald H. Boerum, past President and current Librarian of the Oysterponds Historical Society, was responsible for starting the current effort to print Martha's journal. This could not have been accomplished without the help of many people:

Janet T. Swanson, along with Donald Boerum, proved to be a wonderful decipherer of old writing; she also helped prepare the maps. Charles H. Campbell worked on excerpts from Edwin Brown's log of the voyage, and provided many of the geographical positions for the maps. Mickie McCormic, O.H.S. director has given a great deal of time and support to the entire project. Joan Druett appeared at just the right moment with information, corrections, and a wonderful foreword.

We are grateful to Diana Duell of Orient, her sister Cynthia Hung, and Marilyn L. Reppun of the Hawaiian Mission Houses Museum for their help in obtaining some of the Hawaiian material.

We would like to thank the Bishop Museum in Hawaii for permission to reprint the engraving of the hand cart, and the Kendall Whaling Museum, Sharon, Massachusetts, USA for permission to reprint the watercolors of the *Lucy Ann*.

Others who have helped in various ways are Cynthia Beer, Ann Latham Bliss, Ardis Cameron, David Feeley, Susan Forbes, Paul Hale, Rode Hale, J. Stewart Johnson, Gerald Latham, Frederica Leser, Donald and Hilda McNeill, Sylvia Newman, Gert Reeves, Christine Rendel, Robert Shruhan, Loraine Terry, Reginald Tuthill, Annabel Tyrrell, Gekee Wickham, Freddie Wachsberger, Salley Wiggs and Elinor Williams.

The printing of this book has been made possible by Manuela Soares and Sara Yager, who took a difficult manuscript with nineteenth-century spelling and turned it into a handsome volume.

E D I T O R I A L   N O T E

On August 31, 1847, Martha Brown sailed from Orient on the ship *Lucy Ann* to go a-whaling with her husband, leaving her young daughter, Ella, with relatives. On October 18th, in sight of the Cape Verde Islands, she started her journal. At first she writes to her absent family; later, when she is left in Hawaii to have her child, she speaks to her absent husband. The journal breaks off twice, the first time for the birth of her son Wille— and in the Victorian manner, no details are given to us. Later, her husband's return is delayed, causing her great distress. When he finally arrives, the journal stops. A last page is added three months later. We have included three letters; one from her husband to his brother to fill in the *Lucy Ann's* adventures while Martha was in Hawaii, one from Martha to Edwin while he was away, and one written a few years later by Martha, telling of Wille's death in Orient.

Martha attended school until she was 15, and her writing is generally clear. The age and condition of the journal (which was often written under poor conditions at sea) has made transcription difficult at times. Martha used almost no punctuation, and her thoughts often ran on in very long sentences.

We have added punctuation to make the meaning clear and the reading easier. Victorian spelling was sometimes casual, words being spelled the way they were pronounced. We have not changed her spelling, but have written the correct spelling in brackets if the word wasn't clear. Capitalization has been added, but her own capitalization has been kept. Brackets have also been used to enclose missing words that have been added. Martha's headings for each entry remain as she wrote them.

All the materials have been made available to the Oysterponds Historical Society by Martha's descendants, some of whom still live in Orient. The house that was built for Martha by her husband survives (with alterations), across from the Candy Man store, on Route 25, near the Village monument.

—Anne MacKay

FOREWORD

It is always very exciting to find out about a previously unrecorded female whaling manuscript, but it was a particular delight for me to read the engaging letter-diary kept by Martha Smith Brewer Brown on the whaleship *Lucy Ann* of Greenport, New York, 1847–1849. All of the whaling wives' journals are intriguing, but Martha's journal, kept on passage to Honolulu and then on shore in that place, is more than usually valuable, being such an illuminating document.

All the "sister sailors" were remarkable women. As Donald H. Boerum so perceptively points out in his introduction to this well-timed, deftly edited publication of Martha Brown's journal, women of Victorian New England were a much more resilient and enterprising breed than the popular myth might indicate. In Martha's time, going off with one's husband on a whaling voyage that would span the globe and encompass two or more years demanded a special kind of resourcefulness, however. The challenge was extraordinary. Not only did the sister sailors take up a rough, precarious, dangerous existence, traipsing across the oceans of the world in the company of thirty or more uncultivated men, but somehow thay had to do it without endangering their "true-womanly" image.

In Martha's time the "God-ordained sphere" that belonged to women was very precisely defined by writers such as Sarah Josepha Hale, the influential editor of *Godey's Lady's Book*. "True women" were taught to be pure, pious, peaceable, and patient, and encourged to keep a journal to help the process along. On Saturday evenings well-raised women used their diaries to list what they had accomplished over the week, in a kind of examination of their consciences. Then, on Sunday—the Sabbath, the holy seventh day of rest—a properly pious girl would write down a prayer which was either made up by herself or copied from a book of prayers and sermons that she had read during the long quiet day.

The briefest look at the early part of Martha's journal is enough to indicate that she did her best to conform to this role, just as dozens of other whaling wives did. Like Mary Lawrence, who travelled on the whaleship *Addison* in 1856, Martha listed the pies she had baked and the sewing she'd accomplished over the week in her Saturday entry, and when she was "spaired to behold the light of another Sabath day," she recorded which chapters of the Bible she had studied, and ended her entry with a prayer.

And, as Adra Ashley on the ship *Reindeer* did on New Year's Day 1860, she greeted the new year with a fervent prayer.

There are other similarities. Like Henrietta Deblois on the bark *Merlin,* 1856, Martha went to great pains to describe the bird she saw. Like Almira Almy on the *Cape Horn Pigeon* in 1854, she described the tremendous seas in a storm. Like Harriet Bliven on the *Nautilus* in 1865, she dutifully noted down the ship positions and any major change in the arrangement of the sails, just in case her husband might need to use her journal as a check on his log. Like Malvina Marshall on the *Sea Queen* in 1852, Martha described the fun of exchanging social visits with captains and wives on other ships at sea—what the whalemen called "gamming"—and the surprisingly lavish food that was put on the table for the special occasion.

Sabbath-breaking vexed all the pious whaling wives. Like Almira Gibbs, who sailed on the *Nantucket* in 1855, Martha allowed that it was impossible for a whaleman to keep the Sabbath if there was a dead whale secured alongside the ship, for the blubber had to be cut in and boiled into oil before it went rotten, or the sharks took it first. Whaling on a Sunday, however, was a different matter. Like Lucy Ann Crapo on the *Louisa* in 1866, Martha disliked seeing the boats go off on the Sabbath, and she felt very grateful if the Lord kept the whales out of sight that day. And, like Lydia Beebe, who voyaged on the *Brewster* in 1863, she did her utmost to convert the crew to the ways of religion.

Other wives wrote about the seamen who died during the voyage, many—like Mary Brewster on the *Tiger* in 1846—with deep and painful feelings. Martha Brown's description of the 15 year old boy who sickened and died of consumption on the *Lucy Ann* is particularly poignant, however. "My heart was tuched," Martha wrote, and the reader cannot help but feel touched too. It is also a commentary on the medical limitations of the time, for there was little she could do but give him the promise of a heavenly hereafter if he would only give himself to God, but Martha did that with absolute sincerity. And it says something for her bracingly down-to-earth attitude to life that her reader finds out with a wince that a dying man smells bad—particularly so for the eight men who slept in the cramped, damp steerage quarters with that boy.

Flowery prose was very much the fashion then, and Martha's journal—particularly at the beginning—conforms in this as well. Martha Brown was unusual, however, in her most disarming propensity for malapropism—using what Mark Twain used to call "the second cousin" of the right word—writing "dispersion" when she meant "diversion," and "interposition" when she meant "intervention," and so on. This certainly adds to the fun of reading what she penned—but Martha was delightfully different in other ways as well.

While other wives spoke of their husbands with great respect or even an element of teasing ("grows rather childish in his old age," wrote Harriet Swain affectionately about her husband Obed on the ship *Catawba* in 1854), Martha described Edwin Brown with a wholehearted love that was not afraid to reveal what kind of man he really was. Thus, the reader gains a picture of a man who worried about his men and disliked having to punish them, a man who played the accordian and read poetry, who would bring the ship around and lower a boat to save a kitten who fell overboard.

Martha was equally frank in describing herself. Thus the reader is given a charming picture of this woman picking up her skirts to jump rope on deck with her husband and the mates —"for exersize," she wrote. Likewise, she was not afraid to write openly about her pregnancy. Other wives—like Adra Ashley on the *Reindeer*—wrote about their condition in veiled, modest, ladylike terms. "I am spending most of my time mending," wrote Adra to a friend on February 29, 1860. "... I want to say what it [the garment] was, *but how can I! How dare I!* Well, it wasn't an undergarment with the cuff off but something similar now I guess you will know, and I shall not have to dash my modesty by telling you in plain English." What a contrast to Martha Brown's frank admission that she was making a loose (maternity) dress when she realized that she was pregnant, in February 1848, and her all-too-vivid descriptions of her morning sickness later on!

This, then, was the woman who was left on shore in Honolulu in April 1848, to cope with pregnancy and childbirth alone, while her husband Edwin sailed north for a seven-month season in the whaling grounds of the Kamshatka Peninsula, the Okhotsk Sea and the Arctic. The port where Martha had been left might have been a great deal warmer than the region where her husband steered, but was equally strange: a scruffy, rowdy town of 10,000 inhabitants, where the 600 or so foreigners had a social impact far greater than their numbers might suggest. According to contemporary descriptions, about 1,300 grass houses lined the dusty, straggling streets. The walls of the few stone, stucco or wood buildings were smothered with advertising posters, and an army of mongrel dogs skulked at every corner, yapping at the multitudes of horses that were ridden at breakneck pace about the streets, dodging about the little carts which were drawn by natives and used by foreigners for getting from place to place.

Finding board was a problem for all the whaling wives who were left on shore for the northern season, and Martha was forced to move out to the Nuuana Valley—past the notorious stench of the town slaughter-yards—to live in a wooden house belonging to Mr. John Paty, a retired shipmaster. The board for this was a heavy expense, which marred Martha's sojourn in Honolulu right from the start. She did not state how much it was, but it was probably more than the $8 a week that the Rev. Samuel Damon and his wife charged another whaling wife, Lydia (Mrs. Gorham) Nye, when she stayed there with them the previous season in 1847.

Almost every whaling wife who stayed in the Islands complained about the cost. Food was cheap, but rents, clothes and haberdashery were all very expensive: "gave 50c for a piece of ribbon to tie my bonnet," wrote Sarah Taber in March 1850, and added, "so money goes in Honolulu." The loose shortened "wash-dresses" that were worn on ship-board were not at all suitable for the fast and frivolous social life of Honolulu. For a woman like Martha, with her sensible, down-to-earth attitude to life, pregnant, without friends, lonely and missing Edwin's physical affections as well as his reassuring company, the situation was almost unbearable. It is very understandable that her journal changed in tone there, becoming a very personal document, intended for her husband.

Martha was constantly worried about how she would get along dur-ing her confinement and after the baby was born. Mrs. George E. Young of the whaleship *Abigail* arrived "in similar circumstances with myself" but Martha was not able to call on her as much as she would have liked, because Mrs. Young boarded at the Commercial Hotel and Mrs. Paty did not "associate" with the proprietor's wife, Mrs. Henry Macfarlane.

Not surprisingly, when Martha's time of confinement came, the help she needed was given by a whaling sister. This was Mrs. Slumon Gray, who delivered the baby and looked after Martha and her infant for two weeks afterwards—no easy task, for this was at a time when every new mother was sternly commanded never to leave her bed or even lift her head from the pillow, or else she would be courting puerperal fever. Absolutely everything had to be done for her, from toilet needs upwards, but Mrs. Gray did it all, unstintingly.

For me, this was a much appreciated and unlooked-for bonus of Martha Brown's journal, for it added immeasurably to my knowledge of yet another whaling wife, one about whom I knew a little bit already.

New Londoner Mrs. Gray was the stereotype of a Victorian woman, prone to tears, easily alarmed, and dominated by a dictatorial, bad tempered husband. She was one of the very first of the whaling wives to sail, voyaging first on the *Newburyport* in 1844. In all likelihood, she sailed because Slumon (probably a corruption of the Old Testament name "Solomon") commanded her to do it. Mrs. Gray and child were not left on shore in the Sandwich Island that time, but stayed with the ship for both whaling seasons in the north. Mary Brewster of the *Tiger* met Mrs. Gray in Lahaina when she stopped briefly in Maui, in October 1846, and recorded that she was a "sister sailor, who had been absent [from home] 27 months, [also] saw her little boy who was born on the ocean in Talcahuano [Chile]." This is very interesting, because it is a decided hint that Mrs. Gray was the woman who coined the term "sister sailor", for Martha also began to use the phrase after meeting her.

When Martha Brown met her, Mrs. Gray was on her second voyage, on the *Jefferson*. Mrs. Gray's third voyage was on the *Hannibal,* 1849, and this time she had a baby daughter with her just 6 weeks old. As Donald Boerum astutely remarks, women are just footnotes in history, for men are so much more thoroughly documented. It is certainly so with Captain Slumon Gray. A journal kept on this voyage by the steerage boy, Nathaniel Morgan (now held by Mystic Seaport Museum), gives a detailed picture of a harsh, blustering, unpredictable shipmaster who beat and kicked men at the wheel: "the most profane language I ever heard from mortal lips flows from his," wrote Nathaniel, and added, "His little daughter will accomplish her education young I think, if she is on shipboard with her father."

When the ship "would not work to suit" Captain Gray, he "swore most blasphemously," as Nat Morgan noted. Then the steerage boy added, "his wife begged him not to curse and swear so, and he told her to go below and she would not hear it." Mrs. Gray probably felt the same way Martha did, when she wrote after Edwin flogged a man, "So Mother, you see I have very little influence so far."

In view of this, it was quite a revelation to me to find from Martha Brown's account that Captain Slumon Gray had allowed his wife to stop on shore instead of going north, and—what's more—had given her instructions "to take comfort and enjoy herself, and as far as money and credit would go, not to scrimp herself." Quite a contrast to what I already knew of the bad tempered old salt—and quite a contrast, too, to Martha's own situation.

Martha described Mrs. Gray as very dressy and very social, and perhaps it is not surprising that she should "let loose" a little, after enduring so many chills and fogs on her previous voyage. Maybe she enjoyed herself a little bit too much, for Captain Gray certainly hauled her off up north on her next voyage, on the *Hannibal*. Nevertheless, it seems Mrs. Gray loved her irascible husband. When he lowered in a boat and was lost to sight in a fog, according to Nat Morgan "his wife was alarmed and cried until he came aboard again."

She cried again in June 1850, when the Captain was sick and decided he was dying. The crew, by contrast, was delighted. Gray, however, recovered his spirits and his health when a fellow captain came on board for a boozy gam, and so Mrs. Gray travelled a-whaling yet again, on the *Montreal* in 1853. Then, in 1864, Captain Gray carried her off on yet another voyage, in the *James Maury*. This time he did die. The ship's log records that on Friday March 24, 1865, "Light winds and pleasant wether at two PM our Captain expired." Next day, the crew made a cask, filled it with spirits and put the Captain's body inside. Three months later the ship was taken by the Confederate raider *Shenandoah*, but Captain Waddell was so touched by Mrs. Gray's predicament that he did not burn the ship, but bonded the *James Maury* instead.

Back in 1848 when Mrs. Gray nursed Martha Brown, this was very much in the future—but surely much about the lot of a whaling wife was discussed. Martha wrote too about meeting Mrs. Reynard, who also had a bad tempered husband. According to the account (now held by the New Bedford Whaling Museum) kept by James Worden, one of his crew, Captain William Reynard dealt out floggings daily "in true Virginia style." Mrs. Reynard stopped the previous 1847 season in the Sandwich Islands, and it seems very likely that she had almost as unpleasant time as Martha herself, for Martha wrote that Mrs. Reynard was "not very much liked by the generality here."

It was an unpleasantness that Martha could not have expected. She was ready and willing to cope with all the difficulties of a life at sea, but her pregnancy meant that she was faced with a different challenge altogether. Perhaps it is one of the reasons that Martha never went a-whaling again—or perhaps she made that decision over the long, torturing weeks of awaiting her beloved Edwin's return.

In the event, she was a one voyage sister sailor—but one voyage was enough. The study of nineteenth century seafaring women is greatly enriched by the letter-diary kept by this frank, open hearted, most disarming woman, and Anne MacKay and the Oysterponds Historical Society are to be heartily congratulated for making this valuable and unusual document available to a wider audience.

—Joan Druett, 1993

38 Pearson Avenue
Hamilton
New Zealand

"Right Whaling." Whaleship Lucy Ann *and her whaleboats among Right whales. This watercolor was painted by an earlier crewmember of the* Lucy Ann.
Courtesy of the Kendall Whaling Museum; Sharon, Massachusetts, USA

INTRODUCTION

Martha Smith Brewer Brown (1821–1911) was certainly a woman of her time. The now popular notion that the Victorian woman was a frail and fragile flower subject to fainting spells and the vapors is a far cry from Martha's experience. One has only to begin to examine the lives of the women on the western frontier or the Atlantic coast to see these myths dispelled. The woman who took her family to the mid or far west in order to follow her husband in many instances was left later to work the homestead and raise a family by herself. The plains novels of Willa Cather document this in vivid detail.

In New England, the men who "followed the sea" were sometimes gone from home three or four years. The child rearing as well as most of the farm management fell upon the shoulders of the wife. While the husband was absent, the wife and mother was truly the head of the house.

"Man may work from sun to sun,
but woman's work is never done."

Life for the nineteenth-century woman in a small isolated village was unending toil; bearing children, cooking for extended families and hired workers, nursing the sick, doing laundry, rearing children and seeing to their education—religious and secular. If a woman didn't marry she became a dressmaker, teacher, midwife, worked for her family or "worked out" as a hired girl.

Through all of this a woman held no control over the political destiny of her world. Yet she managed to become the force behind the Bible societies, the mission societies, the temperance societies, the ladies improvement societies and the literary societies—all of which existed in even such a small village as Orient. The experience of organizing and maintaining these groups all over the country would ultimately produce the leaders of the nineteenth-century women's movement.

This was the world of Martha Brown. When Captain Edwin Peter Brown went "a-whaling" for the first two years of their married life, Martha was left to raise their first born with the help of relatives. When she could no longer endure the years of separation from her husband she chose to leave her two-and-a-half year old child home in order to be with Edwin, to go a-whaling with him for however long it took.

When men write histories, women tend to become footnotes. Who knew about the women who sailed the Atlantic and Pacific in search of

Captain Edwin Peter Brown, undated   *Courtesy Oysterponds Historical Society*

Martha Smith Brewer Brown, undated   *Courtesy Oysterponds Historical Society*

whales? Fortunately Joan Druett's excellent book *"She Was a Sister Sailor:"* *Mary Brewster's Whaling Journals, 1845-1851* now lists "443 women— captains' wives, a few daughters, a few mates' wives, a few passengers and four women who went to sea disguised as men."[1] These ships were often called "hen frigates" by the sailors.

Captain Edwin P. Brown was an intelligent, determined young man. The son of an Orient farmer, Deacon Peter Brown, he went to sea at 19, in 1832, as a mate on a coastal schooner. In 1833 he became a boatsteerer on a whaling ship, and in 1841, after a second voyage, he was given command of the whaling bark *Noble*.[2] Although deeply in love with her husband, Martha took no back seat in criticizing his faults. He was parsimonious, and this caused serious problems. Her anxieties about money are deeply felt in the Hawaiian section of her journal and she blamed him for leaving her in inadequate circumstances in Hawaii.

In the 1820s missionaries and whalers both arrived in the Hawaiian Islands. By 1837 the northwest Pacific had opened up as a whaling ground, and the ships began to use the Islands for provision and repairs. By 1846, over 500 whalers recruited in Honolulu alone, and a large community of "sister sailors" joined the missionary wives, looking for accommodations. They had been left there to avoid the dangers of the whaling in the arctic, and to produce children who had been conceived on the voyage.[3]

Martha felt abandoned in Hawaii when she was pregnant. It is possible that Edwin held the common view at that time that pregnancy was the woman's fault: "a man's pleasure and a woman's curse." Certainly the condition was considered so indelicate that it was referred to only in euphemisms. Although birth is a natural event, human childbirth often has many complications.[4] Even in ideal surroundings and with a skilled midwife there were many deaths of mother and/or child. Martha notes in her biography that Jonathan Latham had married Edwin's cousin, Jemima Beebe, for his third wife: his first two wives probably died in childbirth. Many tombstones in the Orient cemetery show a man buried between two or three wives.

Martha lived to return to Orient, rear a large family, and later become the proprietor and manager of one of Orient's most famous summer boarding houses. After his last whaling voyage, Edwin became a prosperous farmer, noted citizen, and one of the owners of the Orient Wharf Company.

Oysterponds, renamed Orient in 1838, situated at the end of Long Island's North Fork, often became an island when the big storms cut off access to the mainland. Insular and self-contained, the mid-ninteenth-century village was a close-knit community of farmers and seafarers.

James Fenimore Cooper (1789–1851), author, seafarer, and farmer, set his novel *The Sea Lions* in "Oyster Pond":

"Plain but respectable dwellings, with numerous out-buildings, orchards, and fruit trees, fences carefully preserved, a painstaking tillage, good roads, and here and there a "meeting-house" gave the fork an air of rural and moral beauty that, aided by the water by which it was so nearly surrounded, contributed greatly to relieve the monotony of so dead a level. . . A farm in America is well enough for the foundation of family support, but it rarely suffices for all the growing wants of these days of indulgence [late 1840s], and a desire to enjoy so much of that which was formerly left to the undisputed possession of the unquestionably rich.... The farms on Oyster Pond were neither very extensive, nor had they own-ers of large incomes to support them; on the contrary, most of them were made to support their owners; a thing that is possible even in America, with industry, frugality and judgment."

Cooper praised the plain speech of the inhabitants: "It gives us pleasure to hear such good, homely, old-fashioned English as 'Gar'ner's Island,' 'Hum'ses Hull' [Holmes' Hole] and 'Oyster Pund'." He mourns the coming of change in the same voice that we hear in the 1990s:

"It is to us ever a painful sight to see the rustic virtues rudely thrown aside by the intrusion of what are termed improvements. A railroad is certainly a capital invention for the traveller, but it may be questioned if it is of any other benefit than that of pecuniary convenience to the places through which it passes."[5]

The seafarers and farmers of Oysterponds were God-fearing Protestants bound together by the fellowship of the Congregational Church. Prayer meetings of various kinds were held during the week and two or more services were attended on Sunday. A smaller but rowdier group lived at the bottom of Village Lane by the wharf, but the upper group had little to do with them. Commerce was growing, almost 20 ves-sels used Orient as home port in mid-century. One of Orient's crops was young men to sail on the coastal vessels.[6]

"Two open Saloons" in Orient began to be a threat to the communi-ty and church, but the Temperance movement, urged on by Edwin's father, Deacon Brown, finally prevailed, and later Orient became a "dry"

17

village. Edwin Brown signed up at the Orient George Washington Temperance Society just before he went to Chicopee to win Martha for his wife. "The year before at the first mass meeting of the Society in the Methodist church, 247 of the 475 inhabitants in Orient Village had signed the pledge."[7] Martha was fortunate to be sailing with a strong captain on a "Temperance Ship." Rough crews and alcohol proved a disastrous mix on many vessels.

What does this life and Martha's journal of her trip around the globe say to the modern reader? First of all the very foundation and cornerstone of her life was built upon an unshakable faith in an Almighty and terrifying Protestant God who showed no mercy to the unrepentant sinner. Time and time again when she had reason to curse her fate, she placed her faith in the Almighty. She shares with contemporary women the fear that she is never "good enough." She plays her role as an adoring and submissive wife, but not without protest. She appealed to his pride as a husband when she informed him that being properly dressed was most important to those with whom she was staying in Hawaii. Martha had been "working" from age 6, and her independence shows in her biography and her journal. When she became Martha Brown, she still retained her Smith and Brewer identity.

It is evident that Martha Brown had a decent formal education. She was acquainted with the standard popular works of literature of the time and well versed in the Bible and collateral reading. Even more interesting was her use at times of French phrases.

From all outward appearances it seems that Martha intended her journal to be read only by her family as a record of an extraordinary adventure. But the work gives the modern reader a wonderful view of the boredom, dangers, anxiety, and fears that those who went a-whaling experienced on the sea, that "great Leviathan" as her husband calls it in his letter to his brother.

Martha was a resolute woman. She bore the fears of terrifying storms at sea. She suffered the pain of separation from her first-born, she suffered humiliation from being inadequately clothed by a seemingly insensitive husband, and the terrors and pain of childbirth under poor conditions. When her husband did not return as expected to Hawaii, she felt it to be the end of her life. She endured everything with a deep-seated faith in an all knowing God, and lived to return to Orient and recount her adventures to her many children and grandchildren.

—Donald H. Boerum, Orient 1993

[1] Mystic, CT: Mystic Seaport Museum, 1992, p.417. The Hawaiian section in this book mentions many of the same people Martha encountered. Joan Druett's earlier book, *Petticoat Whalers, Whaling Wives at Sea, 1820-1920,* (Auckland, New Zealand: Collins, 1991), is a superb history of the women who went to sea.

[2] *In the Wake of Whales: The Whaling Journals of Edwin Peter Brown, 1841-1847* (Orient, NY: Old Orient Press, 1988), pp. 19-20.

[3] *"She Was a Sister Sailor,"* pp. 202, 204.

[4] Major causes of death in childbirth in the mid-nineteenth century were hemorrhage, obstructed labor, eclampsia (toxemia of pregnancy), and puerperal sepsis (childbed fever).

[5] New York: Putnam, undated, Mohawk edition. pp. 6-9.

[6] Information and quotations in these paragraphs are from Richard H. Bliss's introduction and notes to *In the Wake of Whales,* which gives an excellent overview of the history of Orient and how life was lived in the nineteenth century.

[7] *Ibid.*

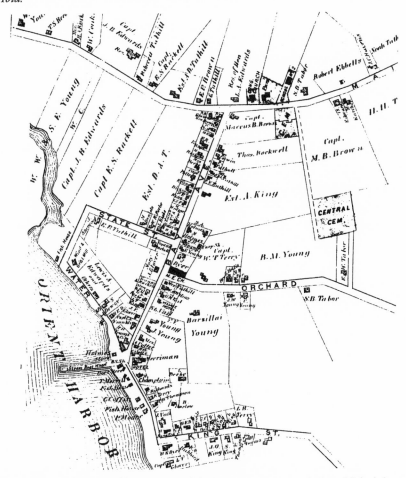

Map of Orient showing Village Lane, and the Brown property in 1873, published that year in Atlas of Long Island.

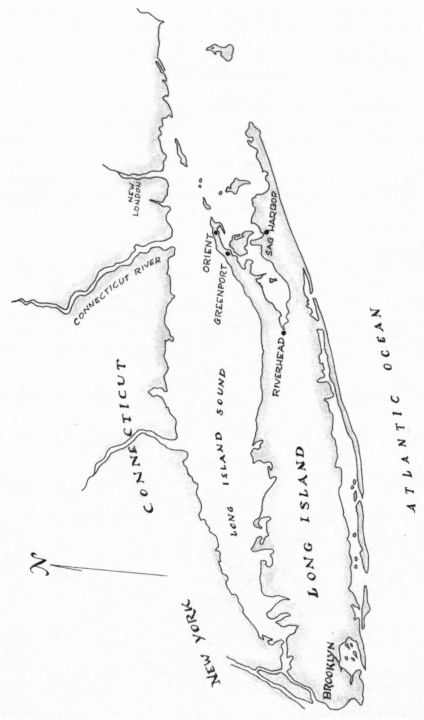

Map of Long Island, New York   *Courtesy Janet T. Swanson*

MARTHA BROWN'S BIOGRAPHY
as told to her daughter
Adelyn Isabella Brown Edwards in 1900

She was born on September 24, 1821, in Southwick, Massachusetts, being the ninth child [of twelve]. When she was six years of age she went to her Aunt Ashley's to live (Mrs. David Ashley's at Ashleyville, West Springfield). Aunt Ashley married her [Martha's] brother. Her life there was not altogether pleasant as her work was hard and she missed the companionship of her young brothers and sisters. She was promised many things if she remained there, which were to be hers at Aunt A.'s demise, but she never received so much as a pin.

She lived there until eleven years of age, when, because of some unpleasantness in the school, her father took her home. About a year from that time her father moved his family to West Springfield to the Ashley house, Aunt A. boarding with them, he running the farm. (The family remained there until December 11, 1839, at which time her father died.) She thinks her Aunt A. told them that they must leave right away, as Uncle Harvey was coming to run the farm. He was married that fall.

Her family moved to Chicopee, Massachusetts. Her mother supported herself by taking factory boarders. She continued at school until her 15th year. In the 15th year she worked at Mrs. Ashley's, a near neighbor (no relation), a few weeks during the summer—doing all the work for the family of 16 & 17, and during harvesting season the family was increased to 30 for a few days! For which she was paid the magnificent sum of $1.00 per week.

That fall she went to her brother Edwin's at Little River, Westfield, to help his wife, and also worked some in the whip shop which her brother (Uncle Edwin) owned. She spent her time between there and her home until July, 1839. At that time, her older brother Harvey had already established himself as a school teacher in New York City. One day a letter came from him. Aunt Patty over in Brooklyn needed a young girl to help her care for the small children, so Harvey asked Martha to come.

To reach there she took the little steamer "Agawam" from Springfield to Hartford (the first steamer she ever saw and it looked bigger to her than anything she has ever seen since.) and a large steamer from there to New York. I have often been amused hearing her tell her experience upon reaching N.Y. —She had no idea where to go, as Uncle H. was to meet her, and he was about an hour late in getting there. She tells how happy she felt when she saw his tall head bobbing up above boxes & barrels as he finally strode down the pier. He took her right across South Street, into Fulton market, where she first met Aunt Patty and Uncle Jake Shaffer, at whose house she was to go and assist in caring for the children.

They lived in Tallman Street, Brooklyn, between Bridge and Jay. Aunt Patty left the market and went with them to Brooklyn, Uncle H. taking her little hair trunk on his shoulder all the way. (It was the trunk at home marked "A.E.S.," Abigail Eliza Smith, and given to Mama by Aunt Eliza.) Aunt Patty got her a good breakfast which she was more than ready for after her first sea voyage and which tasted a little better than anything she ever had before. Her breakfast was chicken and potatoes warmed up together.

It was their last December in Tallman Street that her father died. She received word the 9th of his severe illness and started that night [on the] 9 o'clock steamer from N.Y. to New Haven (she had no idea how to reach her home at that time of the year), and from there by train to Meriden which was as far as she could take the train on her journey. From Meriden to Hartford by stage reaching there by lamplight on the 10th, supposing she could change stages and continue on that night. But because she had no seat engaged she was obliged to remain until the next stage left at 5 the next morning in the pitch dark. It was a stage full of men. The hostelry was the United States Hotel. She tried very hard to have someone give up their seat to her [earlier], knowing her errand, and tried to get up another stage but failed. Her father was alive at that time, and between then and 5 when he died, he was conscious for an hour and knew them all, and left his goodbye for her. Her stage left Hartford just the time he died. She reached there at 10 a.m.

Her life was very happy there [in Brooklyn]. They lived in that house until a year from the next May when they moved to the corner of York and Adams Streets. Captain Robert Brown's family occupied the second floor of the house, as they had also the Talman St. house during the past year. (While they lived in Talman St. they had to carry every bit of water they used for cooking one and one-half blocks from a wooden pump on the sidewalk at the corner of Bridge and Concord.) The families were very intimate and in June, Captin Ed [Edwin P. Brown], who came to New York in a sloop and was a great friend of Captain Robert's, came to visit them.

One Sunday afternoon, while he was sitting in their front room upstairs, she (Mama) went across the street for a pail of water, and Captain

Ed said "Cousin Sarah, who is this?" And she replied "why that is Miss Martha who lives down stairs," and his reply was "By Jolly, she is my wife if I can get her." She, unconscious of anyones being there, went into see Mrs. Brown soon after and "walked right into the trap" (what Aunt Patty said) as she expressed it. True to his resolve he started in that same evening. He wanted her to attend church with him—he was wearing his sailor's garb—but she indignantly refused. She expected a gentleman friend that evening.

The next morning he stopped in to say goodby and that was the last she expected to see of him, as he was to start down the Island by stage. He went as far as Huntington, where his sister Amanda Paine lived, but finding he had left his heart behind him, he returned on Wednesday to try to get it back, or one in its place. He pleaded with her to correspond with him. She would not consent to it. Then he asked if he could write. She said he might and she would do as she saw fit with them. He then left and his letters came thick and fast, from every port he touched and from whalemen whose ships met his in some far off ocean.

A few weeks after this she left Brooklyn and returned to her mother's at Chicopee. This in July 1841. She went to work at dress-making, both going out and taking in, in Chicopee and Westfield, from 7 a.m. to 9 p.m., and wages $1.00 per day.

Sometime between '41 and '43 she and her sister Charlotte visited New York for a few days, but she cannot tell just when. In the meantime, Capt. Ed sailed in the ship *Noble* from New Suffolk—his first voyage as Captain—for a whaling voyage around the world. He returned in the latter part of April '43 and soon found his way to Chicopee. She, that spring, had taken rooms with her sister Charlotte to take in dress-making and children's (boys) clothes. Their communications had been very infrequent and the first she knew that he was on this side of the globe was when he sent a note to her from the hotel next door. He had come with the firm determination to take her away as his bride and and he remained there about three weeks and they were married on May 23rd, 1843, at her mother's home. Her most intimate friends and family witnessed the ceremony—about 10 o'clock a.m. Rev. Mr. Clapp married them and her sister and Mr. Cloniste stood up with them. They [the banns] were obliged to be published at the public meetings in the church. After refreshments, two dozen friends drove to the Springfield depot with them. They were early and stopped at the Massasoit House where they refreshed again. They went to Norwich via Worchester where they remained over night.

The following morning they took a small steamer (she supposes it ran to Sag Harbor) from there, which landed them at Orient Point. Their only way in landing was in a small boat. They had their dinner at the Point House which was then run by Capt. Jonathan Latham who had just before married Capt. Ed's cousin, Jemima Beebe, for his third wife. After dinner he got a small vehicle (which she thinks was truly comical) and took her to his father's home, a distance of three miles. Her welcome from her father-in-law was very pleasing to her. He came in from the field, with hat in hand, and said "Welcome Daughter." Hannah and Libby were unmarried at that time, also Christopher. The best room was dressed up for them in a new coat of white-wash and a new rag carpet which Hannah had woven for herself. Capt. Robert Brown and Aunt Sarah visited them before long and on July 19th, Capt. Ed sailed from Greenport on the ship *Washington,* fitted for two years cruise around the world.

She remained in the family until October when she, with his sister Hannah, went to New York on the sloop *Liberator,* Capt. Tuthill Glover—a trip of eleven hours in a spanking breeze. Hannah visited some relatives and Mama spent about a month between Aunt Patty's, Capt. Robert's, her Grandmother's (Rene Brewer), and other relatives. From there she went to Chicopee where she remained until the next July (at which time she had gone to Little River to visit her brother Edwin), and her husband, having reached port on the 17th, went to Chicopee to see her. (Met on the 19th, one year ago). He got a carriage and with his sister Charlotte drove to Little River. Charlotte left them there and after a brief visit they returned to Chicopee. Then to Orient the same way they did the year before. They drove home and took dinner that day. She thinks they reached Orient the first of August, 1844, and that day Uncle Henry and Aunt Thirza had driven to Greenport to see the first train come into Greenport on the L.I.R.R.

In a short time Capt. Ed left for Wilmington Delaware to look up a ship for some parties he sailed for (Cook & Parsons), and he secured and brought back with him the three masted *Lucy Ann* which was put in to shape in September, or October. He sailed for the North West coast leaving his wife at his father's.[1] Before leaving he purchased the house (known to me as Dell Edward's childhood home) of Caleb Dyer's father for $1,400. The house then stood where the Brown house now stands, only very near the street. The well, which was back of the old house some little distance, is now under the front hall of the Brown house by the sitting room door.

She ate her first meal in her new home on Christmas day. Between the time he left and this time, she had been to New York with his sister Mary and husband John Young and selected her household goods. She lived alone throughout the winter with the exception of a Miss Belle Hill (dress-maker) who boarded with her part of the time. The second floor was rented to Mrs. Lucretia Wiggins with her three daughters, Harriet, Hetty and Caroline. In April Aunt Eunice came to her and on May 2nd, 1845, Ella Orianna was born. Aunt Hannah Havens was married when Ella was three weeks old.

When Ella was five months old, old Aunt E. and Mother went to Chicopee. Their mode of travel was by sloop from here, up the Connecticut River to Rocky Hill and from there by train. The Captain was Lester Terry, and the first mate William G. Corwin. Mama tells of Uncle William pinning the wet diapers to the sail to dry. Capt. Lester's wife was on board also. Up to this time Mother had not been able to keep a meal on her stomach. They reached Chicopee about 3 p.m. and her first question she asked of her mother was if she had any meat. She had not, but got a steak and cooked it and Mother ate heartily of it, and it tasted so good she can still remember the taste of it. She never lost another meal while she was there, and she remained until Ella was 11 months of age, when she returned, her Mother coming with her (April '46). Grandma remained nearly through the summer when Aunts Nancy and Charlotte Brewer came. After a visit, Aunt Nancy returned taking Grandma with her. Aunt Charlotte remained through the winter and Father returned the last day of April, after an absence of 30 months, and for the first time saw his daughter, who only lacked 2 days of 2 years.

In that Fall, they all went to Chicopee and after a brief visit they left Ella in charge of Aunt Eunice and the others—returning by the way of New York. She thinks it was about three weeks, log book says on August 31, 1847, she sailed with Father, from Orient, on the ship *Lucy Ann*, on a whaling voyage.

Another whaler, the *Roanoke*, Capt. Smith of Baldwin, also with his wife, sailed with them. They kept company all the way to Fayal, Western Island, which they reached September 28th, and where they went ashore the next morning. They staid at a hotel two nights and took dinner with the American Consul. They sailed from there Thursday, the 30th, still in company with the *Roanoke* sailing to the east for more provisions, as they could not get much at Fayal. They landed at Terceria, another of the same group. They shipped 72 bushels potatoes (all one ship was allowed to take), fowel, 20 dozen eggs, quarter of beef, baskets of grapes, apples, turnips, 3 dozen watermelons etc., etc.

The wives were taken ashore and had dinner with the American Consul (Mr. Dabney), riding out to his home on donkeys amid much merriment. That was the last they saw of their sister ship. (October 9th when the *Roanoke* left them.)

After rounding the Cape of Good Hope, they steered east and never landed until they reached the Sandwich [Hawaiian] Islands. On the way they encountered a very severe gale (December 19th) in the Indian Ocean in which they lost their rudder. They had to lay to in the trough of a sea for many hours (she thinks as much as two days) while they rigged another. They also had a sailor die of consumption on this trip and buried him at sea. Later they lay to near a little Island, uninhabited, and went ashore hoping to find some fruit, but there was none. They caught a few fish, however, which she said tasted very good.

They reached the Sandwich Islands some time in April [April 15th, log book] landing first at Mawee [Maui] at Lahini [Lahaina] where they remained five days. They had their dinner with some American Missionaries. Their names were Hunt, Armstrong and Richards. They left Mawee the 21st, towards night, landed at nine the next morning at Oahu, Honolulu City. They went right to Mr. Damon's, the Seaman's chaplin, who took Captain Brown back into the valley and found a boarding place for Mama. They went back and had dinner at Mr. Damon's and at 3 o'clock (4 o'clock, log book), Papa sailed for the North West coast, leaving Mama with entire strangers. She remained at Mr. Damon's several days and slept with Mrs. D.'s sister, a Miss Mary Mills. Then she went to her boarding place, Mr. John Paty's. She remained there until November or December, having had a son, William Henry on the 26th of August [August 27th in *In the Wake of Whales*].

Papa came back the last of October with a disabled ship. It took them about a month to get her in condition to sail for home. They sailed from there and went to the Navigator Islands (she thinks Samoa) and staid one night, anyway, with Mr. Williams—whose father, John Williams, was eaten by cannibles in the early missionary days. It was this Mr. Williams who got the natives to dive for Mama and got her all the pink coral in the cabinet.[2]

They sailed from there heading for Cape Horn.

On the 5th or 6th of July [July 7, 1849] the ship lowered a boat off Long Beach and they landed at the Orient Dock on Sunday morning early. (7 months coming, 7 going, and 8 months there.)

[1] See *In The Wake of Whales,* Capt. Brown's log of the voyage.

[2] The pink coral is on exhibition in the Peter Brown Room of the Hallock building, at the Oysterponds Historical Society, Orient, New York.

Martha Brown in front of her house, ca. 1905   *Courtesy Barbara Hughes*

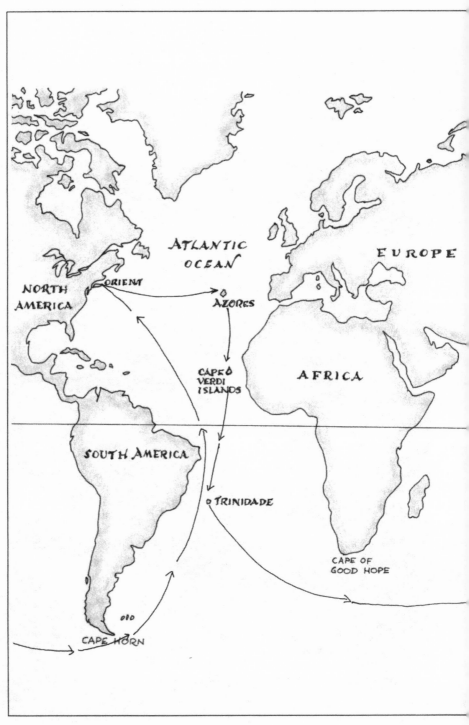

Map of the whaling voyage of the Lucy Ann, *1847-1849*

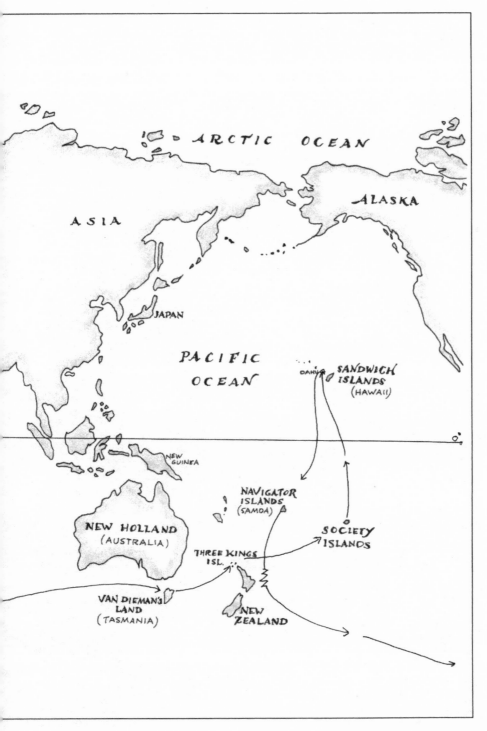

ARCTIC OCEAN

ALASKA

ASIA

JAPAN

PACIFIC
OCEAN

OAHU

SANDWICH
ISLANDS
(HAWAII)

NEW
GUINEA

NAVIGATOR
ISLANDS
(SAMOA)

SOCIETY
ISLANDS

NEW HOLLAND
(AUSTRALIA)

THREE KINGS
ISL.

VAN DIEMAN'S
LAND
(TASMANIA)

NEW
ZEALAND

Courtesy Janet T. Swanson

THE JOURNAL

Whaleship Lucy Ann *of Wilmington. This watercolor was painted by an earlier crewmember.*
Courtesy of the Kendall Whaling Museum; Sharon, Massachusetts, USA.

Monday Oct. 18, 1847

On board ship Lucy Ann. *In sight of the Cape Verde Islands, at sea.*

While you are gradually drawing near and nearer the fire for comfort, I am sitting in my room very uncomfortably warm. I have just come from on deck where the Capt. and myself have been sitting since before the glorious orb of day disappeard in the west. No sooner had his rays departed than the more mild though no less beautifull rays of the moon were pearing down upon us to gladen our hearts, and also to remind us of our afar of [off] home. For on such a night as this it is not unpleasant to think of our friends if we cannot see them, we can in immagination see you [going] to seamens prayer meeting and we would be happy to accompany you there. But since that cannot be, we will content ourselvs with the thought that we shall be remembered (a rair accurance I suppose). If quince groves and moon light nights are incentives to make love,[1] surely moon light nights on ship bord are doubly so. If I was not married I am sure that would be the predominating thought in my mind on such a night as this. We are blessed with musick on evry side: a Portugee concert both vocal and instrumental forward of the try works,[2] and such a rang a tang a tanging I am sure I never heard before. Their tunes have no ups nor downs but right straight ahead. In the steerage they are fiddleing and in the cabin the mate and third mate are practiseing on the accordian and fluit, with now and then a little singing— a variety and also a dispersion. But it is 8 bells and a calm will probily succeed the storm. I do not know how we will sleep tonight it is so warm—I must hasten on deck to get cool. The wind is fair but light, yet we are scuding along at a pretty fair rate with studing sails out. I have been washing, but cannot say much for my cloaths. Think one or two of your jackpants[3] would change their aspect materialy.

> *Lat 16.20 Long 22.25*

[1] Until recent times "to make love" meant courting.

[2] *Try works:* the cauldrons for turning whale blubber into oil.

[3] *Jackpants:* pants tarred for weather-proofing. The name "tar" for sailors comes from this practice.

October 28, 1847

Two months today since we left home and it would be useless for me to attempt to remember what the Capt. has found to occupy the men on deck every day since we sailed: such a round of Coopering, Carpentering, Blacksmithing, Corking, Pitching and Taring, Spliceing Stearing Oars, making Scotchman, picking Oakum[1] and the like I never seed in all my life. Evry one is occupied while I am snugly stowed away in the after part of the ship, siting by an open window nearly two square—sometimes sewing, sometimes knitting, then reading, then attempting to sing—now looking out upon the works of nature, no, of God, watching the birds as they skip not from bough to bough but from wave to wave, admireing the wisdom that gave being, and prolongs their existance where there is naught for them whereon to light save the deep blue sea.

And now I must be disturbed in my peacefull abode by the Carpenter, who has come to do me the favor of making the dead light[2] tight, to secure me from the intrusion of water, when in some after day the good Ship *Lucy Ann* may be strugling with the raging eliments that would fain engulf her forever in her deep caverns.

The weather is very warm, uncomfortable so and I do not know what would be more acceptable than a good drink of cold water from the north west corner of the well. Christopher[3] will you get me one? Martha.

[1] *Coopering and corking:* making barrels for whale oil.

Scotchman: material placed over a rope to prevent its being chafed, also, a wooden strip to keep dishes from falling off a table.

Picking oakum: loose fiber obtained by untwisting and picking old rope—used for caulking.

[2] *Deadlight:* a strong shutter outside a porthole.

[3] *Christopher:* Captain Brown's brother.

Friday Oct 29 ➤ *lat 6:20*

It is almost a calm, and as a matter of course the Capt. is fidgiting and worying about getting on the whale grounds in season, and now and then a little cross grane, especialy if evrything does not go right on board. He was rather blue the other day when he got fast to a large sperm whale and lost him. For my own part, I could not win a smile—then I recollected I had come a whaleing.

34

Today I have been making pumpking pies and I heardly think they can be beat if I had nothing but water and Eggs to thin them with. I have made four kinds of pies since we have been out, and none of them were dried fruit. I anticipate useing them [the dried fruit] when they will taste very good. My sweetmeats keep finely as yet. Oh for one sweet kiss from my Dear little Ella—it would be far more preacious than gold. Why did I leave her at home? Had I known I should have [been] as well as I have been, I think I should never [had] been persuaded it was best. She would have beguiled many a lonely hour for her Father as well as me. It is nessesary to go one voage to know what we want. I think the next time I shall enjoy it much better. At twilight, the hour for putting her to bed, I have no other amusement but walking the deck, looking at the water, occaisonaly droping a tear or two by way of relief to my anxious mind.

Saturday, Oct 30,
➤ *Lat 6 = 57, Long 22 = 04*

Today has been very pleasant, but warm, with no wind to speak of, and that little ahead. This afternoon we went on board the *Peru,* of Nantucket. Visited with Capt. and Mrs. [Consider] Fisher—spent the time very pleasently. For supper had roast pig, Apple pies, Gingerbread and cheese. who could ask for more—they appeared to have evry comfort they could ask for. The ship had been thourly repaired, evry thing looked new and nice and very pleasent, but she was much smaller than the LA [*Lucy Ann*]. Consequently, her motions were more quick and not as pleasent to one that was seasick. Capt. Fisher gave me a nice little black pig so, you will persieve my live stock increases fast. We have now a goat, a pig, a number of fowls, two ducks, three cats and a rabbit. But the worst of all, the stewart [steward] killed all of the roosters before we knew it. We miss their crowing very much, which is very pleasent at sea, and last not least I have a severe head ache to close the day with.

Sunday 31,
➤ *Lat 5=36 Long 21=15*

Through the interposition of divine providence, we are spaired to behold the light of another Sabath day, and, though we cannot today enjoy the privilages of the Sanctuary, God grant that its sacred hours may not be misimproved in the closet.[1] Nothing can debar us from comeing to God in secret, and have we not the promice that he will ever hear the cry of faith and penitence, and in his own good time and manner send gracious answers of peace. Evening. I have read the first 4 chapters of Matthew with the explinations and notes in the Cottage Bible,[2] and anticipate going through them regularly. Read 4 chapters every Sabath aloud for our entertainment and instruction, with a fervent prayer that God will bless them to our spiritual and everlasting good. Edwin has read two cantos in Mr. Robinson's Poems, which we find very interesting. It is my desire that Jesus may be our spiritual teacher—that although deprived of the stated means of grace, which I especially have hitherto enjoyed, we may not be left to grope our way along in darkness, but be ripening for heaven as we are advancing towards the grave.

[1] *Closet:* a private room.

[2] *Cottage Bible:* (New York: Connor & Cook, c.1800-1877).

Monday Nov 8, 1847

With propriety I think this can be called a rainy day, for it has rained almost without cessation since morn and for nearly 24 hours, so that I have not been on deck today untill after supper, and then the decks were very wet. The Capt. came down today looking rather down in the mouth. I asked him what was the matter. "Oh," he says, "it will do no good to tell you," but, after a little coaxing, he said one of the forward hands had taken the ranes [reins] in his own hands and been slaping a green Portugee,* which he had several times repeated, and he was deviseing a plan how to put an end to it. How he proceeded I have not learned—probily he was sent to mast head to scrape and slush down the mast—that seems to be the usual resort, and I am thankfull that mild means answer as yet. Edwin is playing on the accordian and I am going to knitting which is my evening occupation. Martha

* *Green Portugee:* untrained Portuguese sailor.

Monday 15th

It is now two weeks since have written any. Dureing that time we have been through various scenes—we have had a number days of almost perfect calm, gamed [visited] with the ship *Midas* of Nantuckett,* Capt. [David] Eldrige. The same day we took the south trades, have crossed the line [the equator], and are now making tolerable good headway towards the Cape of Good Hope and thence through the Indian Ocian. This is the best part of the story. We will glance at the other side by way of rememberance and say good night. Dureing two weeks we have had one man in the rigging for playing cards and stealing tobacco to pay his losses with, and Saturday, to crown all, a large rail fell from the carpenter's bench and broke one of the white kitty's feet and an old hen's leg. Oh Dear what next? M.

➤ *Lat 8=22 by Long 30-22*

* *Midas:* of New Bedford, not Nantucket.

Thursday, Nov. 25

Today we have a cracking brieze and have glided through the water at a rappid rate. It is very pleasent, after several days of almost perfect calm, to see the ship again crowded with canvass speading her way like a thing of life. This morning, the Island of Trinidad* was in sight and the rocks of Martins [word not clear]. About 10 o'clock we were directly abrest of the latter, not more than 5 or 6 miles distent. They had a very imposing appearance. There were three seperate rocks descrnible from the ship. The largest looked from the ship to be as large as a very large building. The next in size looked like a large hay stack in shape, and about the size. As we passed it we percieve there were other small rocks attach to it. The other one was much smaller and [had] neather forme nor comliness. I find there is much to interest an inquireing mind on the Ocian, anthough [and though] it has been called a dull, unchangeing Ocian, I think, however, that is not correct, for it is continually changing. One day it is spread out before us—a sea of molten glass. The next, it is running mountains high and lashed into a perfect foam. But among all the changes and varietes, I have not had the privilage yet of seeing a whale along side. At present, that is the highth of my ambition. The 15 [?] while blowing rather strong, we carried away the fly gib boom, the first accident of the kind that has happened since we left. The next day the weather leach of the fore top gallant sail parted and away went the sail half way acrost. Another job of mending for the sailorboys. By the by, they have had plenty of that to do since we have been out. About the same time, one of the white kittens got thrown overboard. The Capt. brought the ship immediately round, lowered away a boat, and caught her agane. She came on board pretty well drenched, and from apperance somewhat fatugued, I should immagine. I washed her off in fresh water, and she has survived the disaster, poor thing. I have washed and ironed and mended, this week, two weeks washing—and suned our trunk of best cloths and the Capt. chest of everday ones, hoping they will stay aired for some length of time.

➤ *Lat 20.40 S Long 28,57*

* *The Island of Trinidad:* Trinidade, a small island off Brazil,opposite Rio de Janeiro.

Friday 26

Very light winds, and those directly ahead with frequent showers. It has cleared off to night but no prospect of a fair wind. O that we may not be left to murmer or complain, but feel that what ever God does is right. We have a young man on board that is sick. I fear he has got the consuption,* and has but but a little while to stay with us. He is not 16 years of age and has no hope in Christ. Poor soul, far away from home and friends, sick, no kind physician to precribe a healing balm for his diseased body. But what a consolation that Jesus, the grate physician of soul, is evry where presant. And that he will, if asked, enter the gloomy uninviting forcastle or stearage of a whale ship and administer the healing balm of consolation to the wounded heart. I think he desiers to become a Christian, but I fear it is because he thinks he cannot live long. But be that the case, nothing is imposible with God, and I hope and pray that he will truly convert his soul. I went into the stearage this afternoon to give him some medicin, and asked him how he felt. His answer was, "Mrs. Brown, I feel bad." He complained of a pain in his breast and said he was cold, althoug buttoned up with a monkey jacket on. My heart was tuched. I came back to my stateroom and gave vent to my feelings in a flood of tears. But what could be done—we have but the one room. The Capt. sent for him, and he has spent the afternoon and a part of the evening in here. He can have no comforte here, but if his hope was stayed on God, all would be well.

* *Consumption:* tuberculosis.

Saturday, 27

We have had the wind fair to day, but very light, and are making slow progress—an emblem I fear of my progress in the cause of my blessed Lord and Master. O that I may daily grow in grace and be constantly ripening and preparing for heaven. I have spent the day sewing, making a few pumpking pies, and cleaning my little room. I trust I feel thankfull that my health is so good as to enable me to perform these little acts, and in that way administer to the comfort of those around me. Martha

➢ *Lat 22.26*

Sunday 28.

Unworthy as I am I have been spaired to injoy the privilages and blessings of another Sabbath day, while thousands, who can do more good than I can, have been called from time into eternity. My tallents are small, but I must give an account of my stewardship, that I may improve them so as to render up my account with joy, and not with grief. To whome much is given of him much will be required, but does that in the least lessen the obligation of the steward who posesses the one tallent? No, certainly not. I have been reading the memores of Mrs. Winslow, mishionary to India, to day. And when I think what she done and suffered for the good of souls, and still felt to be so unworthy of the name of a Christian, and to come so far short of her duty. What can I think of myself, sitting with my hands folded and apparrently thinking—that I am to be carried to heaven on flowery beds of ease? I think I have enjoyed my mind more today than I have before in some time. O that I might feel the worth of souls and have grace and confidence given me to warn sinners to flee from the wrath to come. We have need of a mishinary on board. We number 31 in all, and not one, I believe makes any pretentions to religion. And as near as we can ascertain, not but one in the forcastle that can read, out of 16. I feel that I desire to do something, but know not how to begin. May the Lord guide me. I will look to him alone for direction.

➢ *Lat 24.05 south*

November 30

My mind is gloomy and dejected. It appears as if I was in darkness—thick darkness that could be felt, as it were. O that Jesus would appear in our midst, and quicken our souls, and ennable us to do our duty, and let our light so shine that those around us may be led to honor and glorify God. I long for more confidence that I may speak a word in reason. If we loved Christ as we ought, I think we should always have something to say for him when we are or are not in the company of his professed children. I often think (and the thought condemn's me) how often we met together in our sewing society. Spent three or four hours together and parted without once mentioning the subject of religeon, the subject, above all other, which ought to lay nearest our heart. I feel now if I am ever permitted to return and meet with you agane, I will endevour with the help of God to be more faithfull. Immagin, you who love God and delight to see sinners comeing to Jesus, what must have been my feelings but a moment since, to hear that poor sick boy pleading with God to have mercy on his soul for Christ's sake. His tone and petition was humble. I cannot but hope Christ will appear in his behalf. Have had some conversation with him today, and the Capt. has tonight. Think he is truely seeking, and if so he will surely obtain. His feet commenced swelling last night—no very good sympton. It is very hard to see him gradualy growing worse and can do nothing for him. If he was a Christian how different—into God's hands I commit him and all will be right.

> *Lat 27-05 S Long 26.17 N east*

December 2, 1847

Oh what a kind and gracious Saviour, ever ready to forgive sin and except [accept] of us into his fold. This evening, as the Capt. and I were siting in our room, John came to the door and called to us, and said if we were not to buisy he would like to come in and talk with us on the subject of religeon. As soon as he had sit down, he said he felt better in his mind today. He felt that God had forgiven his sins and would except of him as [his] own. He said he had been reading the Bible and praying and he felt as if he loved the Saviour, and loved evrybody. He thought he loved his enimys as well as his friends. The Capt. asked him if he could give himself into the hands of God. He answered very promptly, "Yes sir, I feel raidy to die any time he sees fit to take me." Oh, blessed hope, what is not religeon

40

worth? It is my sincere prayr that he may not be decieved with a fals hope. If he has truly given his heart to God, all is well. We united in prays [prayers] with him. I have felt burdend on his account for nearly two weeks, but more espicialy since last Sunday. I have raid much in the Bible and prayed often, for I felt that all was in the hands of [God], but my prayrs are week and feeble. To God belongs all the praise. It is my sincere desire that that it may not stop here; perhaps God hath grate things in store for us. O that we may be fervient in prays, ernest in spirit, serveing the Lord.

➢ *Lat 29-41*

Friday morn 3

I had some conversation with John Wednesday evening. He seemed to regret that he had come to sea and expressed a strong desire to get home to his friends agane. Last night he said he was almost glad, not almost, but he felt glad, that he had come to sea. He felt as if that was the way God designed to bring him to himself. He thought if he had staid at home he would still gone on in sin, and perhaps lost his soul. I asked him Wednesday if he did not feel that he could commit himself into the hands of God, and let him do with him as he thought was right. After a moments pause, he replied he did not think he could go to heaven with the heart he then had. I asked him if he did not wonder now how he could so long been unconcerned for the subject of religeon. He said he thought of the many privilages he had slighted. He wished he could be in a revival of religion—he was 3 years ago. I read to him a number of paseges in the Bible, among others the theif on the cross, with the explination. And told him God was not confined to land, neather to revivals, but when we could give our selves up as did the theif, feel our own unsufficintcy, and feel that Christ was all sufficient, that was all he required. How easy the tearms of salvation look and live. He has spoke of his Sabath school teacher—thinks he would rejoice to heare that he had given his heart to God. M.

Saturday Dec 5.

Very good weather, considerable wind and fair, We have had no severe gales since we have been out—some that I thought would answer to be called little young ones. I would be satisfied if we never had any hearder ones, but expect evry day and night to see the waves running mountain high. I feel, however, as if I could trust myself into God's hands, and feel that all will be right. Nothing in particular occured to day interesting. The cry of "There she blows" was heard this morning. Ship under full sail, took in sail, brought the ship to, loword to [lowered two] boats—first and second mats [mates]. No success, whales going to the windward faster than they could row. Returned to the ship and breakfasted about 9 0'C. I have done up a little Saturday's work and this afternoon sit down. Slicked up both myself and parlor, felt quite at home, but wanted Ella, bless her little heart. Oh the sweet child—dreemed of seeing her last night. At first she was a little shy but come to me, I took her in my arms, asked her if she knew her Mother, called her Mother's sweet creature as I was wont to do, walked away with her but she soon put up her little lip. I gave her back to Aunt Nancy and of course put up my lip to [too]. Another Saturday night has come upon us. One week more gone into eternity, and soon it will be said of us—gone into Eternity. M.

➤ *31.20 Lat*

Sunday 6, 1847

[written in margin: "Albatross"]

Today has been about as unpleasent, or uncomfortable, as any day since we left home. The sea has been rather boisterous—more so than any day before, and it has been quite cold for the first time. I have longed to sit down by a good fire. We have kept our room shut up close and still I have been obliged to have some thing around my sholders. It has come very sudenly. Last night was the first time we have anything more than a sheat and a window open. To night we want a comfortable [quilt]. I saw an Albatross today for the first time. Hope we shall soon see one on deck; I have quite a desire to examin one close by. Have given some tracks [religious tracts] to some of the crewe and requested they might read them attentively. O that God would bless them to them for their spiritual good. Had some coversation with the mate—feel to desire earnestly that he may be led to see the error of his way and feel his need of Christ. Feel to mourn my own imperfection and short comings and especially my neglect of duty. O God may I be more faithfull and live nearer the throne of grace.

Saturday 11. 1847.

The past week has been diversified with various changes. Sometimes an almost perfect calm, then a good brieze dead aft, now a smashing brieze. The ship close haul on the wind, occasionly the welcom sound of "Their she blows'" which would prove to be nothing but a fin back.[1] Birds are very plenty, a viriaty of sizes from a large Albatross down to mother carys chickens. Yesterday I saw a speckeled hagget[2] very near the ship. It is a beautiful bird when seen manuvering at a little distance. I have washed, Ironed and mended. Made a pair of pantilloons for Francis[3] and fixed another pair of large ones for him, and made a flanel shirt, and have another one to make. Beside nitting consiterable and spending one day fixing up my wollen stockings. Now I think that is doing prety well. By the by, this week has been rather cold. I have kept closited in my room most of the time. Of cours I have much time for medattation; my mind is often absent from the body and in imagination I call on one and another, grasp the extended hand, exchange the kiss of affection, clasp my Dear Idolized babe to my heart, and for a moment feel blessed and happy. Such bliss is of short duration and then, as I have hundreds of times said in regard to Edwin's comeing, I sigh and exclame audibly, though alone "Have patience and if our lives are spaired we shall meet some day." Cool consolation—but such is mine and has been most of the time for five years. When will these things have an end. It is eight years today since I looked upon the cold and lifeless form of a beloved Father. How vivedly do I remember the feelings I then had. This earth was to me but a blank. It appeard as if evry alurement was withdrawn, and my only desire was to depart, for my treasures were in heaven. But how far have I wandered from the fountain head of all happiness dureing those eight years. Have I lived as though I expected to meet my Father there? No, I have been an unprofitable servent and have not made that advancement in the Christian corce [course] it has been both my duty and my privalage to. I look to God for his blessing and guidance that the 4th year, if I am permitted to spend it on earth, may be more fruitfull and more subservient to the glory of God. Amen.

[1] *Fin whale:* poor in oil and whalebone.

[2] *Hagget:* Speckled haglet, shearwater, a bird of the open sea.

[3] *Francis:* possibly Mr. Sisen, the first mate.

Sunday Dec 12. 1847

The holy Sabath day has agane passed with its privilages and blessings, but I have not felt that peace and joy I have for a number of weeks past. And why, have I done my duty? So that must be the cause, for God is the same yesterday today and forever. I fear I have performed my closet dutys as a task instead of a privalage, and have neglected to warn those around me of the danger of liveing in sin. O God give me a truly penitent heart for this days neglect, and enable me to be more heavily minded for the future. We have had a very good wind, not much, but fair, and the sea has been as smooth as a lake. There has been nothing to prevent an uninterrupted intercorse with God if the heart was only right for the service. God grant to purify and sanctify us for the grate work that is before us. Amen.

Monday Afternoon Dec 20—1847.

[In margin: "waves mountain high" "lost small boat"]

Praysed be God that I have once more the oportunity of siting down with pen in hand to scribble here the events of the past week. Nothing in particular occurd the first part of the week. We spoke an English Merchantman Tuesday. The Capt. sent a boat on board to get some papers he proposed to give him in hopes to learn something of the war,* but all to no purpose. He sent him a buckitt of potatoes and some pumpkings. The English Capt. offered to return the compliment by way of sending a little rum, which the mate very politely declined accepting. Thursday it commenced blowing pretty strong from the westward. It continued to increase dureing Friday and Saturday, and Sunday morn it blew very hard. They were obliged to take in some sail before seven bells. It continued increseing gradualy untill noon, when it blew an almost perfect gale. Between one and two they close reefed the main topsail, took a reef in the forsail—the only sails there was on the ship, and it may with propiety be said the waves were running mountain high. It is astonishing to what hight the wind will cause the water to rise in heaps. I did not venture on deck all day but went several times and stood on top of the stairs in the companionway. Sometimes there would be a huge wave on either side of the ship, another ahead and astern, and the ship in a deep valley. The next moment we would be mounted on the top but to be plunged agane in the depth. Well has the Psalmest said they mount up to the heaven.

44

They go down agane to the depth—their souls are melted because of trouble. They real to and frow and stagger like a drunken man. They are at their wits end, then they cry unto the Lord in their trouble, and he delivers them out of their distresses. Oh that men would praise the Lord always for his wonderfull works to the children of men. I felt to posess the spirit of drowning Peter and with Childelike confidence to exclame "Lord save or we perish." About two o'clock the spair boat lashed on the stern was carried away with a number of spare spars, a large oak plank. A dozen or 15 pumpkings and several other things went high and dry. It was a solemn time. I would think sometimes we are all here now—but where will we be the next hour? God only knows. At such a time without a firm reliance on that God who holds the winds and waves in the holow of his hand, what miserable creatures we are. It looks truly frightfull to see some 8 or 10 men laying on the yard furling sail, the waves a rowling, the ship a pitching to and frow, and the winds a howling. It appears evry moment as though they would certainly be thrown off. About 5 P M brought her to the wind, took in all sail except the foretopmast stay sail and foot of the close mizin, and we lay roaling in the trough of the sea untill morning.

* *The war:* Mexican-American war, 1846-1848

Wednesday Dec 29

Captain Smith of the ship *Cadmus* came on bord and spent the day. It was very pleasent, but am sorry to say he was no temperance man—but so far from it that he asked the Capt. if he was not a going to fetch on any thing to drink. This was what he called a "dry gam" [non-alcoholic visit]. He seemed to think he would rather see his Wife to day than a sperm whale. For several days have been somewhat unwell. Have had a verry bad turn of colic, but feel better today. Have thought much of my dear little babe and perfectly longed to see her.

➤ *Lat 42-26 Long 45 = 22.*

January 1 1848   *Ship Lucy Ann Indian Ocian*

I wish you all a happy New Year. We have had a very pleasent New Years day. Yesterday I made 2 nice plumb cakes, and a large molases cake, and we have had my little black pig. By the way he was nice and fat, and made a good meal for all hands aft and forward. They had soft bread and butter and apple pies. The question is, do we feel thankfull to God for his kind and watchfull care over us? He has brought us through dangers seen and unseen through the past year, and permitted us to enter upon this new year. Let us endevour to be more faithfull the present year, for this may be our last. We have one in our midst that I fear can live but a little while. We thought he would not live out Saturday night but he appears somewhat better now. He cannot speak aloud but little of the time. He called to us this morning through the bulkhead and wished us a happy New Years. We could just decern what he said. He has uncomon good courage, good spunk. The steward says he smels very bad. The boatsteerers whose berth is over his, has taken his bed and gone into the sailroom. He cannot sleep so near him. He is in the stereage where there is 8 men beside himself. It makes it very bad. What frail creatures we are; we can look on him and learn our own mortality.

➢ *lat 43 = 16 long 52 = 23 East*

Monday 3

This morning fine, pleasent, and but little sea on—something so unusual since we have been in the Indian Ocian that I had courage to undertake a four weeks washing. But before I got half through it blew on so that I could heardly stand to my tub, and in squals I hung out my cloths. But the Capt. had to take them in, line and all, together in a short time before they had dried any. And there they stand in the basket, fast to the line, and my wollen clothes in the tub on deck in the round house. Oh the troubles of the married life especialy at sea. Hope on hope ever, hope for the best.

➢ *Lat 44=55 Long 58=00*

Wednesday 5

Yesterday it blew very hard all day. Sometimes it rained, sometimes it hailed. No chance to dry cloths. Hove to at 2 A M and lay untill this morning. We put out the clothes, they have dried after a fashion. Have been wet a number times with showers, and some of them a number times with salt water, but must make the best of it and anticipate better next time.

➢ *Lat 44=30 Long 65=38 East*

Monday 10 [in margin: "John died"]

This morning about 7 we were called in the stereage to witness the departure of an immortal soul. He died very suden. The Capt. went in imediately and he gasped but once. He never strugled, nor groned nor to appearance mooved a musle. He said last evening he felt that he must die, felt prepared, and was willing to go this morning. At 6 he told Steward he thought he could stand it to get to New Holland [Australia]—he did not have his reason all the time. A short time before he died the boy said [he] heard him singing and laughing. He is Portugee and could not understand him. We think he might have been happy, but we do not know. It is not probile he knew he was dying. He never left a mesage for his friends although the Capt. often asked him if he had not something he wished to say to them. I heardly think he would have given us the names of his parents or friends of his own accord. He was young, only 15. I hope he has gone to a brighter and happyer world, but that we can not know. We will leve him in the hands of a just God who doeth all things well. He was buried this afternoon at 4 oclock. It was a sollemn sight to see his body launched into the deep. I think nearly evry one wept. Oh that they may lay it to heart and realized their turn will soon come. They are far from being what we would wish them to be. They have looked rather thoughtfull today and I pray the impressions may not be banished as soon as his body is out of our sight. Poor boy, I cannot realize he is gone. Poor in the world estimate, but if he had sincerely repented of his sins and was truly a child of grace, how much richer far than we who remain behind. Whether he felt any dred of being buried in the sea or not, I do not know. He did not say any thing about it, and we did not mention the subject to him, but it matters not where the body is if the soul is prepared for heaven, prepared to meet its God.

> *Lat 43 = 20 Long 87= 20*

Thursday 13 [in margin: "ate porpossis"]

Today I have the unspeakable pleasure of seeing a whale brought along side. The second mate struck him. I was on deck most of the time they were off, notwithstanding it was somewhat rainy. It was past 7 when they came on board, and after getting dinner it was to late to cut him in. Like wise it was blowing pretty strong so we were obliged to lay by him all night. It [is] quite encourageing to think we have got one of the thirty of forty we have got to get, ere we can anticipate returning home. It looks like a long day I can assure you to look ahead to the time when this ship shall be full of oil and we homeward bound.

➤ *Lat 42=40 Long 93=10*

Friday 14

Morning rather unpleasent but commenced cutting in about 10 AM. And of cours the Capt. worked hard. Evry time the ship roaled, the whail went nearly all under water, but they succeeded in getting him in at 9 pm. Weather quite good. Got supper, cleared up, but have not commenced boiling yet.

➤ *Lat 42=50 Long 93=00*

Saturday 15

Called the Capt. between 5 and 6. Lowered for whale—no success. Commenced boiling before breakfast but have not made very grate headway. Will be under the necesity of boiling tomorow, Sunday, but I do not see how whaleman can in evry way keep the Sabath. They can truly not go off in the boats and take them, but if they have one alongside or in the bluber room, it appears necessary they should take care of it.

➤ *Lat 43=23 Long 95=15*

Monday 17

Today hands imployed brakeing out the fore peek and stowing down 42 barrels of oil. Merely a nest egg. Hope they will have the good luck to get the nest full soon and set the sails for home. Finished boiling this morning about day light. It has been very pleasent all day. I have been making my blue dress after supper. They caught two nice large porposses—now for a feast on fresh meet agane. By the bye it goes well.

➤ *Lat 49=40 N*

Wednesday 19

Another pleasent day and I have improved it washing. Had a good time. Got my cloths dry before night, but lost one apron overboard—the first time I have had the bad luck to loos anything. Got through little, afternoon. Had fried parters [potatoes?] as turnovers for dinner.

➤ *Lat 44=50 Long 101=35*

January 23, 1848,   *Indian Ocian, Ship Lucy Ann*

To day has been a lovely day, a good breeze and a compleet day for whaleing. The Capt., I think, has been quite anxous to see whale. The first time he has been to the masthead [on] Sunday, but he who know all things saw best not to tempt them. And here I will add we have not seen a whale on Sunday since we have been out. How kind is Almighty God to withhold temptation when there is not strenght of mind sufficient to resist it. I fear and tremble evry week that we shall see them but it is my earnest prayer that God will be gracious and tempt us no further than we are able to bare.

The 23 of Jan was my dear Father's bearth day. If he was living to day he would be 68 years old. But as our heavenly Father saw fit 8 years ago to remove him from this world of trouble, sorow and pain, of which he alwayss had his share, to one we trust of perfect bliss, happyness. He can never more come to us, but we can go to him. Then let us strive to meet him in heaven, dear brothers and sisters, for that is our privalage.

➤ *Lat 43=40 Long 120=76*

Monday 31

Nothing in particular to day. Strong brizes from the west. In the morning at 2 am raised Vandieman's land [Tasmania], but at so grate a distance it appeared like a cloud. Nothing was visable and of course we were not much interested. I think I should be nearly intoxicated with delight if I could once more get ashore where I could feel at home, and go as I was a mind to—for instance on Long Island. But let me get ashore any where, I anticipate I should enjoy it some.

➤ *Lat 43=42 S Long 147=49*

Tuesday, Feb 1st

Ship Lucy Ann Between New Holland & New Zealand Feb 1848

Today has been quite pleasent, and it is very acceptable to think that we may now have some good weather, for it has been nothing but a succession of gales and bad weather since we left the cape of Good Hope. But if it is not one thing is another. Sunday morn when the Capt. first got up, he went on deck and caught to [two] of the foremast hands fighting, in direct oposition to the rules and regulation of the ship. He sent one out on the bowsprit and the other to the mizenmast and kept them there untill 10 oc [o'clock] without their breakfast. It was their watch below. This morning, or before noon, he appeared at the fore castle—lo and behold there were four gambling for tobacco. Two managed to get rid of their cards so that he could not know certainly they were playing, but the others said they were. Seaman he sent out on the bowsprit agane, for he was the one sent there for fiting [fighting], and Rider to the mizenmast head. Kept them there all the forenoon, their watch below agane. In the afternoon he called them of [off] aft, read to them apiece on the results of gambling and lectured them full a half hour, threw their cards overboard. Agane, at 8 bels in the evening Baldwin, one of the boatsteerers, came with a complaint that Seaman had been calling him a horred name—the third offence three days a runing. The Capt.'s patienes was clear gone—he went on deck and gave him 5 or 6 lashes with the end of the topgalent bowlin. Then for the first time I learned he had floged a man several weeks before. What will come next I do not know. You who live on land do not know half the trials a sea Capt. is subject to. If you do not like a man's conduct you can pay him and let him go, or you can flee to the law. But here there is no such thing. Of course there must be some rules and regulation on board ship. When a man is made acquainted with them in the first of it, what can he expect but abide the conciquences if he does not abide by the rules. So Mother, you see I have very little influence so far.

➤ *Lat 44 =09 Long 149*

Friday 11

This morning at daylight raised two Ships, one of them cutting in. At 8 PM raised three Kings,[1] steered for them. About 2 PM sent two boats ashore to see if any-thing was to be got in the way of provision. The third mate soon returned with the chief, said there was plenty of potatoes and that was what we wanted. He came abord to make the bargain with the Capt. but more expressly to get some Rum. They could not land that side of the Island we was, but this kanacker[2] came down the rocks some way. The Capt. made a trade with him, sent them back. But by this the current was runing so strong and the wind ahead, the second boat could not get around, and was obliged to land the Chief where they took him. So the third mate walked across the land to the other boat, or the landing place, to have Mr. Sisen take the potatoes. But mean time he had come around, thinking the Capt. had not sent him back. When they got on board nothing had been seen of the other boat, and of course we imagined the boat had swamped and all were drowned. But alass [at last] they come and brought 10 little pon fish. This ends our tour of the three Kings.

[1] *Three Kings Island:* on the north end of New Zealand.

[2] *Kanacker:* Kanaka, general term for a Polynesian man.

Saturday Eve February 12

And so we are spared to enjoy the privalages of another Saturday night, and if we cannot meet with our friends at the temperance meeting nor in social prayer, we know that our Savior is present to hear our feeble petiton if offered in faith. What a blessed privalage. I think at times what could we do here without the Bible and the family alter [altar]. I long to live nearer to God and enjoy more of that love. It is our privalage to do. I have to mourn daily my coldness of heart, ant [and it] appears the more I strive the more I see my imperfection—and short comeings. Today has been very pleasent. Very little wind, some of the time almost a calm. It is warm and I spend most of my time on deck. The Capt. is aloft a grate deal of the time and it is lonely below. I have just come from the deck where we have been jumping the rope for exersize—The Capt., my self, and the mates—nice sport.

> ➤ *Lat 33=46 S, Long 174= 40 East*

Sunday 13

This has been a lovely day. A pretty little brieze with three studen sails out, and we have been moving at a midling rate. But with all this pleasentness we could not enjoy the privalage of hearing the sound of the church going bell, nor of assembling ourselves together without it in the house of God, to hear dispensed the words of truth and life. And if we were like many or most of our crew, would not read a word for ourselvs. Methinks our condition would be a deplorable one. What better are they than the poor heathen, especially hear at sea? They have appeared very well so far on the Sabath, they make but little noise. But what they do in the fore castle I can not say. The Capt. has not had to reprimand them once, I believe. I have proposed reading to them. Some of them say they would like to hear good reading. I desire to put it of [off] no longer than next Sabath if it is pleasent. The Capt. thinks he cannot take up his cross for he says he has no one to help him, which is very true. But I trust the Lord will help him, then surely he will be helped. The mate tries not to believe in anything, but still he has a heart, and I trust one that is susceptible of right and wrong, and a Wife that is a professer of religeon. And I hope he will ere long join her heart and hand in her heavenward journey.

➤ *Long 177=20 E*

Monday 14

Today has been almost a perfect calm, we have not moved enough to be sensable of it. This morning we discovered a ship and have been steering towards eachother all day, and have not gained enough to acertain what nation she is of. Just afternoon the Capt. took a notion to pull aboard to exercise his boats crew, but more I think to brake the spell. Since 4 we have had more wind, have come more togther. The mate has just come on board and proves to be English. I am quite anxious to have the Capt. come home—the longest he has been absent since we left home, about 5 hours. It is dark so I will stop.

Tuesday 15

Today we have had consiterable more wind. It has rained—A little gust last night and we have prospect of a gale. They have been furling sales and sending down the main royal yard in anticipation. The Capt. returned just after dark, and Capt. Baker came with him to get some shoes. He and the mate took 5 pairs. Capt. Baker gave me bottle of wine, one of oil, one of porter and a nice peace of fresh pork roasted, which was quite a treat I can ashure you—for we have not had any fresh meat since we have been out but once. But I have not got to loving salt joinck* yet.

> ➤ *Lat 32=35 Long 179=68 E*

* *Salt junk and hardtack:* salted meat with flour and water biscuit were given as the sailor's normal food in Helen E. Brown's *A Good Catch,* (Philadelphia PA: Presbyterian Board of Publication, 1884.)

"A Right Whale Breaching." Whaleship Lucy Ann *and her whaleboats among Right whales. This watercolor was painted by an earlier crewmember of the* Lucy Ann.
Courtesy of the Kendall Whaling Museum; Sharon, Massachusetts, USA

Sunday Feb 20

Another of those pleasant days—so inviting on that seems to say come out and worship God. And I trust many are engaged today in that most delightfull of all imployment, not in form only but in sincerity of heart. For why not praise and adore him here as we shal in heaven? If we are ever so happy as to praise him there, there will be no desembling there, but be known as we shall know, and see him as he is. We have a very long rain storm since I wrote last, but not much of a wind gale. The wind was ahead and blew pretty strong so that we took in sail most of the time. But now we have a free wind and are sailing along very pleasantly. I am longing for something good to eat. That is my greates trouble at present,

Monday 21

We have had a very pleasent day, good brieze, and I have been washing and of cource am pretty tired. For you know it does not agree with sailors to work, and I must confess that I am as lazy as any of them. It is near three weeks since I have washd, for want of water. But today had plenty good soft rain and I have reveled. Steward has been cleaning pantry and making pumpking pies. On deck they have been mending fore sail, cleaning binicle, carpenter mending companionway with the Capt.'s help, and other things to various to mention. So good night.

February Wednesday 23, 1848,   *South Pacific Ocian*

Yesterday and today we have had good strong winds from E.S.E.. Stearing NE by N. And I have employed myself below sewing, fixing an old dress into a loose dress [maternity dress], and mending up all of Edwin's old cloths for him. On the Northwest, for we are drawing near the Sandwich Islands [Hawaiian Islands], and there he is bound to leve me. They are painting and varnishing up high on deck. I think when they get through it will look very nice, and then we shall be happy to wait on any of our friends. The old Preacious is in quite good spirits. A fair wind. He sometimes mourns for that Sperm whale that took his line and another right whale they had spouting blood, but uppon the whole he is very patient, and I cannot but think there is good luck for us some where yet with percivereance.

<blockquote>➢ Lat 27, 37 Long 163,28</blockquote>

March 2, 1848

Some where in the nabourhood of a group of Islands. Anticipated seeing Oratongo [Rarotongo] Sunday or Monday without fail. But we have been dodging back and forth from north and nor west to south ever since—untill yesterday when the wind hauled so they could stear about East insted of north east which he wants to. Now we make a E south East course. When we shall ever get to our destination I do not know. I have been sick all this week so that I have not done enough to earn my toast the Steward has made me most evry day. O dear O dear I do not want to go to sea, no that's what I don't. And if we ever live to get home agane we won't eather in my humble opinion. I think I shall be glad enough to have a respit at the Island, if we are so fortunate as to reach them. I am not sorry I come, however, if Edwin must, but Oh I want my dear baby, my darling Ella.

<blockquote>➢ Lat 29—27 Long 159-00</blockquote>

March 8

It appears you can have no Idea how warm, or how hot rather, it is. There is heardly bit of comfort to be taken but on deck, and that we have not had the privalage of enjoying untill today for it has rained every half hour for a week. And I forgot last night to note down what a ducking I got through one of the side windows. I was sitting directly under it, open—the ship roled her side under, and I gues full a pailful of water struck me on my head and wet me to my skin. Then, after supper, I was on deck and a sea broke over the ship where I was sitting. No alternative but I must sit and take it. In the evening, the Capt. went up and another sea broke over him, weting him completely so he was obliged to shift him [change clothes] through out. Another comfort we have is bed bugs, but I will tell you more tomorrow.

<blockquote>➢ Lat 15-35, Long 156-59</blockquote>

March 9 1848

When shall we ever get any where where we want to? Heading N. West by W on on one tack and S.E. on the other, when we wish to go N.E. or there abouts. I have tried to encourage Edwin untill I am nearly out—I know not what to say to him next. I have had strong hopes that we might get home in 22 or 24 months at the fartherest—I will try to hope still, but it looks dark. Is it not useualy darkest just before day? I fear we are not thankfull for what blessing we do have. I pray that we may be, and remember that all things are ordered by a wise being who knows what is best for us at all times. Yesterday was Edwin's bearthday—35 years. As the pact says, just half way from the cradle to the grave, should he live to arive to the appointed age of man. How few do, in comparison to those who die younger. O that we may ever have our lamps trimed and burning, wating the comeing of our Lord and master. For fear that while immersed in darkness—thick darkness—we hear the cry "behold the Bride groom cometh, go ye out to meet." But while we examine our hearts to see if it is us that are called, the door is closed, and closed against us for ever. I fear there is many who are anticipating a blesed entrance who will never reach the celestial city. O God help me to search my heart diligently that I may not, at last, that I may not be forever thrust out.

➤ *Lat 4-49, Long 157- 49*

March 25

Well here I am agane, waked up after 3 or 4 weeks, and making a feeble attempt at writing, trying to wory a little down [eat something]. I have been sick most of this week and by dint of hard labour have only made one shirt with short sleves. I have catched as many colds as there is days in the week, and nights to, for all what I know, and have come to the conclusion that if I go on deck and open my mouth I am sure to get a new addition. The gray cat was missing last week for several days, and one day they found her dead between two casks. Poor creature she come to a miserable end. She was a pet with all on bord, and I was sorry to part with her, for when I see her I use to think about Ella's pulling her about the house by her tail, and many other sorts of game they use to enjoy together. But she is gone, and my sweet Child where are you? O that I could know this moment. They have got nearly through painting the ship, but when we shall get to the Sandwich I [Islands] is yet to be acertained. We are crawling along slowly. The Old ship leaking 800.50 strokes [pumping] a day, and the Capt. fretting about it, and about the wind, and about getting on the northwest coast, and about getting a voyage and about getting home, and O dear me, "O dee me" as Ella use to say.

➤ *Lat 2-11 Long 149. 50*

April 2 Sunday Eve

We are yet many days sail from the Sandwich I unless we have better winds. We will keep hopeing althoughe each day brings the same disappointment. I have not been as well the past week. My cold has been very severe in my head. Have felt better today I think than before since Monday, when I washed on deck, which put the climax on I calculate. I have been reading Mores Practicle Piety and Cause and Cure of Infidelity the past week. Have been much interested in them—Nelsons, in particular. If I could remember what I read I think I might become much wiser. It is my wish to become wise unto salvation I wish all cavillers [detractors] of the Bible could be persuaded to read that book and follow his direction for a happy result. Might we anticipate?

➤ *Lat 7-31 N Long 148-15 West*

April 30, 1848   *Sandwich Island, Honolulu. Oahu,*

It is one week yesterday since I agane took up my abode on land, and two weeks since we arived at the Island. One would think I might feel very well contented here after the 7 1/2 months residence at sea, but it is not so. I am less happy here than there. This is not my home and I do not know of one here that I can call my friend. They all appear very kind, but what have I to reccommend me to them. The one that can dress the best, and make the most show is thought the most of. In that respect I am far in the back ground. It is my earnest prayer that I may be contented with my lot, but my hard and stuborn heart will rebell aganst the better dictates of concience. I am at home alone, have not availed myself of the privalage of the sanctuary. Although the day is quite pleasant, the wind blows very hard and occasionaly a sunshine shower blows down to us from the mountain. Oh my wicked heart it appears as though I could not have one good thought today. If I read the Bible or other good books, they are dull and uninteresting and all I feel inclined to do is to meditate on my lonely situation, and contemplate the dark side of evry thing. Forgive me Oh God, for Christ sake, the sins of this day and all my past life, and create my heart anew, that I may love the more and serve the more faithfully. Incline my heart to do thy will, and help me to banish pride, envy, and a desire to please the world far from me, and help me to desire above evry thing else to enjoy the favour of God and feel assured that my name is enroled in the lambs book of life. I feel that I desire this far above all the wealth and splendor by which I am surrounded. I did not feel well enough this morning to go to church, and it is so far that I cannot go this evening. I wish I was down town on that account, but I trust all things are ordered for the best by a wise and benevolent God. This Sabath has not been spent as I like to spend the Lord's day. Mrs. Paty had company to dinner, and one who did not belive in the bible—his conversation was anything but interesting. I had a nap since dinner and dreamed of you, my dear, and Ella for the first time, I think, since you left me. Oh how I wish I could kneel with you to night at the throne of grace.

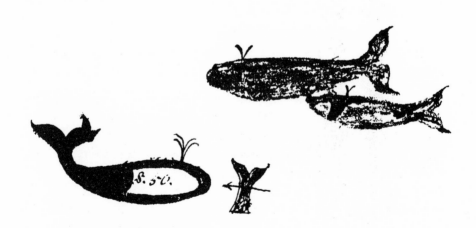

Drawings by Captain Edwin Brown from his logs.

[On May 7th, Martha wrote the following letter to her husband:]

Oahu Sunday eve May 7, 1848

My Dear Husband,

With pleasure, I embrace this first opportunity of sending to you. Since you left I have been very unhappy most of the time since I left the ship, but begin to feel more contented now. And were my expenses less, and my circumstances different I think I could pass the time of your absence very pleasently—but still I would perfer being on board the ship. I spent the Sabath at Mr. Damon's,* Found them a very pleasent family. Went to church twice, morning and evening. Heard Mr. Damon in the morn, Mr. Atkinson in the evening. Mr. D.'s subject was the wonderfull perservation of the shipwrecked company on Christmas Isle—and they arived all safe to land. The text you will find in Paul's shipwreck. He refered to the ball, and regretted they had not been as zelous in returning thanks to God, as to the officers of the Sarcelle.

The Monday before noon he brought me up in the valley, and his natives took up my trunk so that it cost me nothing. The next Thursday was Parlement. Wednesday afternoon Mr. Damon and Miss Mills rode up to see if I would like to go, and in the morning came up after me. I took dinner at his house, and about 4 pm he ried me home. The next Sabath I did not feel very well and did not go to church. Mrs. Gilett came up to Mrs. Paty's Tuesday morn, after I went there and staid two days. We of course sympathised with each other, and tried to console each other, but on one point her endeavours were fruitless.

Last Wednesday afternoon she and Mrs. King, one of the new mishonarys, came in Mr. Gilett's waggon after me to return the visit. I spent two nights. Thursday afternoon the Ramehameha *had returned with part of the mishionarys, for I saw Mr. Thurston's family, Doct. Andrews, and numbers of others. Friday morn I got raidy to come home although it was raining hard in the valley. (By the by, it has rained almost every day since I have been here and is raining now.) But as the school closed at Punahow that day, and I had an oportunity to go, I turned my attention that way and spent the day very plesent. Saw a large number of the mission children together, and also the mission families, among the rest Doct. Baldwin's. Mrs. B.'s health is improveing, they some anticipate returning to Lahina, but Mrs. B. said they had* laid no plans for the future. Mrs. Gilett and myself dined at the establishment at a table with 10, and at the second table there was over 40 children—an amusing sight. I can assure you they behaved very prettily, and on the whole, I think the Mission children far excell the children of other forreign families here in behavour. They passed examination admirably. Sung several times and at the close, sang "Farewell to Punahow," an origanal peace to the tune of Auld lang-sine. After the examination closed at 5 oc, I returned to Mr. Castle's, expecting to return into the valley by means of a hand cart drawn by the natives. But Mr. Damon came for me with his horse and waggon—which happened very well for it rained in torrents a part of the way, and I should probily got very wet, but did not.

With him today I have been to church in Mrs. Paty's cart with two natives, one before, and one behind, her little girl went with me. It cost me a shilen [shilling]. I heard Mr. Hunt preach from the words, Jesus Wept. Mrs. P. has had company both Sabbaths since I have been here once to dine and today to tea, which is not pleasent to me, you will of course conclude as I cannot shut myself up from them. But I staid in my room most of the time today, but I can hear almost evry word spoken in the parlor as the partition is nothing but canvass, and an open space at the top of that. But I think it will not be so much of the time. They are acquaintinces from California, and the vessel sails this week—or expects to.

And now my love, it is past 10 oc and I must have prayers without the well known voice of my husband. But although we cannot mingle our voices together on earth, the same ear will hear our petitions and let us be encouraged to come in faith and spread our wants before Him. Good night, Dearest, and may your sleep be sweet, and may you dream of me—a privalage I seldom enjoy to meet you or Ella in my dreams. I think we are not to Old to kiss. And agane good night.

May 14

It is Sabbath afternoon agane, one week since I commenced writing to you. But as there has been no oportunity to send, I have delayed finishing it. But now I expect to [have] two chances this week and shall endevour to send it by them both. There was an arivle here the 11th, *Ship* Abigail. *Young and Leady in similar circumstances with myself. They called here on Friday to get a place, but Mrs. Paty could* not accomidate her, nor inform them where they would be accomidated. I heard last night they had got a place to a Mrs. McFarlen, whose husband keeps the commercial hotel. The caratter [character] of the family I know nothing of. Mrs. Paty said "I am sorry she has gone there for I should like to call on her but but I shall not go there." I said "why?" "Oh," she says "I do not associate with her." I shall call on her the first oportunity, but it is a grate effort for me to get down town. I have been down three times in the hand cart, once of a week day, and twice to church, and have been near sick each time. I want to go down tomorrow but do not know how I shall make out. The Canada, Capt Ranard, expects to sail on Tuesday, and I am indebted a call to Mrs. Ranard and give them this letter. Also for your own dear self. Capt. arived on Thursday and last night came to anchor outside, for what reason I know not. Mrs. Young expects to be confined next month. She appears to feel very bad, poor woman. I can sympathise perfectly well with her.

By the by, I am getting very well contented and getting along finely. It takes me most of the time to fix my dresses so I can feel comfortable with them on when I go out. Perhaps you will think me extravigent for buying me a shall [shawl] but I have done so one—for 6 $, a very handsom looking thin shall. For last Sabath I was asshamed truly of my silk one. It looks rather shabby I think in a strange place, even for a bluberhunter's wife, and rather than enjoy the the luxury of having my washing and ironing done, which would cost perhaps a dollar a week, I have got a shawl. And you will remember it was your doing that I did not bring my crape [crepe silk shawl] which I very much regret, although it would be rather warm. It looks well and that appears to be the mane object here.

But this is not a subject for Sunday, and I will close as my sheet is full with the hope of writing another to send by Young, if I can ascertain when he goes. I shall number my letters as I write them, not because I expect to send so many, but that you may know if there are any on the ground [whaling grounds]. My dear Husband, do not cease to pray for me daily, and you shall never be forgot. I long to know what sucess you have met with. Adieu for the present. M.

*Samuel C. Damon, 1815—1885. Sent to Hawaii in 1841 by the American Seamen's Friend Society. He was pastor of the Oahu Bethel church for 42 years.

STREET VIEW AT HONOLULU.

Street View of Honolulu, showing the hand cart, 1840

Engraving by A. T. Agate. Courtesy Bishop Museum

May 11, 1849 [1848]

Time is passing swiftly and I can not say that I regret it. In 11 days more, one of the 7 months will have passed, which I trust will be one 7th of the time of our seperation. Our Daughter's bearth day has passed since you left, and a homesick day it was, I can assure you. I could think of nothing else comparatively but that precious little one. she has if alive, my Dear, commenced the fourth year of her earthly exhistance. How can I realize it that I am a mother of one so old, when it appears but a short time since I myself was but a child. But so it is, and Oh that I may have wisdom from on high to enable me to discharge my duty as a Christian Mother. Martha S. Brown

May 21

The Sabbath has agane dawned upon us and passed, numbered with those before the flood. I have been to church today, but have felt so unwell I fear I have got very little good if any. Mr. Atkinson preached. A young man who is to sail on Tuesday with his wife for Origon—she is in like situation with myself. I think they feel bad about going, for the Indians are murdering the white families there in numbers in that vacinity,* But no doubt their trust is in God. He appears like a decided Christian. Mrs. Damon was confined last night a son—I think a daughter would have been more pleasing. I wish I could say that I to had a son, but I desire to wate God's time. An interest in your prayers I trust I always have. With this beliefe I close.

* *The Whitman Massacre:* Marcus Whitman, American pioneer and missionary. His Mission was attacked by the Cayuse indians November 29, 1847.

May 23, 1849 [1848]

[Martha's wedding anniversary]

Five years ago today.

(Six years married May 23, 1843)

June 6

The natives came for me at 9 oclock, and I came in the valley yesterday. I washed and was verry tired and suffered very much from my old complaint. Today I have ironed, but have not felt much of any better— am afraid I shall be obliged to give it up but shall not as long as I can do it. For I have been reconing up my account tonight since I have been here, and am astonished at my expences. I do not think however I could [have] done any better, I have got no dress, neither do I intend to, nor have I got any for the expected one. And, my Dear, I fear your Wife will make rather of an indifferent impression upon the minds of the Honolulu residences, but she does not let it disturbe her hours of sleep.

[The next paragraph appears to refer to some early difficulties about financial matters.]

If I can retain the heart, the undivided affections of my husband, it is all I ask. I can not forget but I can forgive. Yes, I have forgiven, and forgive me for refering to the subject. But I often think of it, and must own it causes me many unhappy hours even at this late day. Since I have had so many assurances of yours that your heart is still my own, I think sometimes, perhaps his heart is mine, but he would perfer his money himself, and I certainly should perfer you to have the disposal of it, Dear. But under present circumstances what am I to do? Some times I feel very unhappy, at other times I think would this have been my situation had it been contriary to my Husbands wishes? And agane did you not object to my fetching nice sheets and pillow covers, and also clothing for myself? Now, for one unguarded *moment* we must abide the consequences and let us do it without murmering. I the pain and anxiety, you the expence. Were it not for my expences and realizing in a grate measure your loneliness, I should be very well contented, for the time of our separation is decreseing, and I feel that 6 or 7 months will not be 30. And then, oh the happiness of being agane clasped in your loveing imbrace. Oh my love, I see families here that appear to have evry thing heart can wish but they do not appear to have that love which to me appears so escential to happiness in the married state. Good night.

Sunday Eve, June 25

This is the second Sabath I have spent at home from church. Two weeks ago to day I went, and when I came home I felt very unwell, and was almost afraid I should make a mis-carage, for it was about the seventh month. I spent a very unhappy night the first part of it, at least. I felt better about midnight and went to sleep, but I have been very carfull since and am obliged to be on account of my complaint, which I fear is a assumeing a more serious form. If I keep just still, I do not feel it much— but a little exercise on my feet, and especially walking, brings it on directly. It seems rather peculur to this climet, as many foreign ladies here are troubled in the same, and some are obliged to ware a supporter. They cannot live, or rather walk, a step without one.

Monday morn. I hope, if I am carefull, not being obliged to be upon my feet much I shall get over it. Oh how much I want to see you and have you see me. You would take very little pride in my form at present, unless it was because people would be led to judge that you was "miki," as the natives say. I have just finished reading the *Mother at Home*. I think it is an excelent book and would prove a safe guide for every mother who would follow its precepts. What a pleasure it would be to me tonight if I could undress our darling little one, and hear her lisp her infant prays, recieve her good night kiss, and then lay little head upon her pillow. In two months I shall probily have that duty to perform for the one yet invisable, or a part of it at least, and I do not know as I care how soon after I get my things in raidiness. Mrs. Young was confined the 15 of this month. I saw her on the 20, she was very comfortable. Her babe weighed 4 lbs—Mrs. Carter says 2 ¾ [?], she affirms its cloths weighed 1 ¼. From my appearance I think I shall beat that, but I do not care how small it is if it is perfect, for I think there is more room here for it to grow than where it is now. Hers is the third baby with in a month. Mrs. Abels is the other. Mrs. Gilett has gone to Toawhi* and I feel rather lonely. She enjoys being here much and well she may for she has traveled over the whole group of Islelands and is at very little expence, too. I am sure she came from home well fitted to stop here. But adieux.

* *Towahi:* Hawaii, the largest Island.

Sunday July 2, 1849 [1848]

I have spent the past week rather pleasently. Have been down town most of the week staing at Mr. Damons. Mrs. Gray has arived here from Hedo, or Hilo. She spent the day at Mrs. D.'s Wednesday and also a Methodest Mishonary and his wife and family from Origon who are here waiting for a pasage to the States. There names are Brewer and we of course have traced out a connection. We are both decendents of the Springfield Brewers. Capt. B. is also a distant connection. He belongs to the Salsbury family. The new Chaplain arived also on Wednesday. They have been over 8 months from home, but have stoped at several different ports and were 5 weeks of [off] Cape Horn. Mrs. T. has not been well since her arival, she has a slow fever. They met Mr. Thurston's people here, heard Mr. Tailor preach this morn from Titus 2:14. Was much pleased with his discourse, also his appearance in the desk.

Mr. D.'s people speak well of him as a man—from what they have seen of him like his appearance much. I think he is quite inteligent, and a man of good education. The mishionaries have all returned to their stations. I had but little of seeing them while here—was pleased with those I did see. I am so far from the mission nabourhood and also from town that sometimes I am rather discontented. By the by, Mr. Hunt is coming here to reside, and I am in hops I can get in with them. I like Mrs. Paty very well herself, but the accomodations are not what I could wish for the price I pay. But perhaps I can not better myself—I intend trying at least. I have felt rather more unhapy yesterday and today than usualy for a variety of reasons. But what is the use of letting the crosses and vanities of this life intrude upon the hours set apart for the service of God? Help me, Oh my Father to collect my wandering thoughts, and for a few moments forget the world and its trials and temptations, and hold communeion with my Saviour and friend, blessed privalage. There I can come with confidence and make known all my wants and feel the assureance that I am heard in heaven. I sometimes feel to be near my Husband and Child, from whome I am separated by land and sea.

There seems to be a connecting link between those we love. It is getting late but were I writing to send to you, I think I could postpone sleep an hour or longer without much inconvenience. I hope I dream of you tonight.

Monday

Oh Edwin, what a consolation it would be if I could be in your embrace of sweet contentment. I sigh for that state room which you occupy, or for our L.I. home, or anywhere but here as I am without wealth, beauty, or fashion. I have no heart or means to join them. I received a long call today from Capt. [name not clear] who is here repairing his ship.

[the ink on the final paragraphs is so faint that the words are not legible.]

Tuesday 4

Yes the 4 of July has agane passed, and how think you love I have spent the day? Not as I did the last in your society, and with our Dear little Ella, but alone. Yes, truly alone. In the morning I washed. Mrs. Paty went down town to a lunch. I and Fanny sat down and dined alone, after which dressed myself hoping I might recieve a call from Capt. Spencer and Mrs. Gray. But on Mrs. Paty return learnt she was to the lunch. My thoughts have been far from here today and would that in body I was with you. Just of my lonely situation but when I am permitted to take up my abode on ship. Well.

Wednesday 5

Capt. Spencer and Mrs. Gray have called today and sit sometime. The Capt. entertained us for nearly an hour with a narative of his troubles at Hope Isle. Poor man, what narrow escape. It is enough to chill ones blood to hear it, and what must have been his feelings! I sincearly hope my Husband will never have such a tale to reherse to me, as he will have to tell Mrs. S. on his return. He was married when home last, has his wife's minature. It is very pretty looking. I regret very much that I am up in the valley. It cost so much to go down often, and then I can not see my Sisters but seldom, for so we call ourselves. Mrs. Gray says to me to night when she left, "Oh how I wish you was down town so that we could see eachother often." She says, "I do not like the society here." Neather do I, and if I was not in family way, I think we would spend but little time here for we could travil about the Island much cheaper than we can board in Honolulu. But we must pay dear for the whistle this time love, and it is my earnest prayr that the little stranger may be permitted to live, for I must own my disappointment would be great and not more so, I trust, than your own. He is lively enough at present, of that I am certain, and if I continue to increase I think I shall be eaquil to Mrs Damon in size—but I hope better form. Her boy grows finely. That we may both be watched over by our heavenly Father this night is my earnest prayr.

Sunday 9

I have not been to church to day and have not spent the day as proffitably as I could have done on board ship. I fear it appears as if I was getting farther and farther from my duty and my God evry day I live. I cannot be retired, that is imposible here, but I do not wish to excuse myself wholy on that ground. It is my wicked heart. Mrs. Paty went to town this eve, and I was left alone. But your profesional brother, Capt. Smith, saw her and learnt that I was alone, and took pains to come up and spend the evening with me, for which I was very thankfull. I had just been crying, and could not conceal it from the eye of a stranger. Even he remarked that if you know how unhappy I was and lonely you would not probily feel very well satisfied. True my love, if you knew how unhappy I was here you would wish me with you, almost regardless of the consequences. Oh how often I think of you in your quiet little room, and if I was there to give it a brush now and then, would it not be pleasenter? I know it would, and if I ever am permitted to be there agane I can never consent to leave it untill you do, and I hope that will be on the shores of Long Island.

Monday

10 oc. I have been washing and have been through an hour. Was very tired for I had a large wash. If I did not have to pay so much for my board I would get it done, but as it is I feel obliged to do it. I think this afternoon of going down to see Mrs. Gray, but have but little courage to do so, for it is very warm here now and do not feel as if I could dress my self so as to appear heardly decent. But I must stop writing for my heart is swelling fast and it will soon burst over. I am afraide my child will be cross and worysome—for if there is anything in the feelings of a mother during preagnancy, I am sure it will be so.

Thursday 13

Mrs. Gray has been up and spent a night with me. I found her a very agreable companion. We have both got a new dres and are making them. Don't say I am extravagent—mine cost $2.00, hers $ 5.50, both muslin. She has 5 new ones, and if I got boarded as cheap as she does I would have more, for I need them badly. Tomorow I expect Capt. Spencer up after me to return her visit. The time I think will pass more pleasently in her society, and I regret very much that we cannot be together. But as I hope to be folded in your arms in a few months, to hear you say we will not part agane, love, I will be contented or try to at least. So good night and pleasent dreams.

Thursday 18 [20] Private

Have just returned from Capt. Hoyer where Mrs. Gray. is boarding. Have spent the time very pleasently. Capt. Smith brought me up in a Carraige, which is much pleasenter riding than in those little hand carts. I have been and got me a new dress, another muslin. I wish you was with me so that you could get them for me, but I need them very much and as I cannot ask you to get them for me, perhaps you will alow me to do it. I feel very sorry to have to spend one dollar except for my board, which is extravigent, but no more so than some of the rest. Capt. Gray told his wife when he left her to try to take comfort and enjoy herself, and as far as money and credit would go, not to scrimp herself. She is not in circumstances. My Husband left me in one of the most unpleasent situation a Lady can be left in, without her husband, and among strangers, with the request that I would do my washing myself—a thing which no other American Lady does, not even the mision Ladies. That however, I was willing to do as long as I was able. But now I am not, and I do not know as my Husband will pay for it willingly. You also requested that I would not buy any thing but what I positively needed. I think I have done so, and when I realize how much money I have spent, I feel very unhappy. Oh, Oh, Oh, that I was rich, but that can never be. But I beg of you, my love, that you will never place me as I am agane, for I feel evry day almost that I recieve slights because I cannot dress in silks and nice cloths. Before Mrs. Gray came I felt alone. Now I feel that in her I have a true friend, although she far exceeds me in dress and show. She knows her husband would wish it therefore why should she hesitate? Capt. Smith did not wish me to come up this week as he expects to sail next Monday, and he thinks it is pleasent to come in and spend the evening with us. I do not know how it is with you, but I know that I wish I was with you on board the *Lucy Ann.* There I should not have to spend anything.

July Sunday 23

I have been to Church twice today. Captain Spencer came up after me in Mr Damon's wagon. The children went with me. I went after the morning service, to Capt. Hoyer. At 4 o'clock Mrs. Gray, myself, Smith and Spencer went to hear Mr. Hunt—the first time I have heard him. He has quite a congregation. He preaches at present in the Charity School House. I think he appears very much engaged for the good of souls. I hope he will do a great deal of good—there is need enough of it I am sure, for I think the forreign residence [residents] need a Mishionary more than the natives at present. His family are stoping at Mr. Castles at present, as they can not get a house to live in. I have called upon Mrs. Hunt. She has not returned it yet. I returned home in Mr. Damon's wagon about sundown. Mrs. Gray rode up with me near Doct. Judd's house. Capt. Spencer says "Oh here," and took out of his vest a small scrap of news paper, and what think you was my surprise to read the death of our Dear Sister Mary.* I had mentioned her at Mr. Damon's— Miss Mills recollected her name. Saw the account in papers they recieved by the *Matilda* or brig *Mary,* I think which sailed later from Boston. Had it not been for her I should not have known it. When Spencer went for the horse and wagon she gave it to him to give me. I wish you could be here to [word missing] church occasionally.

Sister Mary: Edwin's sister, Mary Brown Young.

Monday 24

Capt. Smith called this eve. He expects to sail this a.m. tomorow. He appeard very down hearted, his owners have failed. He has been to considerable expense—has had to botomray* the vessil I should think, he said, and has been out so long. Said when he sailed he had not $100 to leve with his wife, and if so that his agents or owner had failed, did not know how she would get along. Had some money which he wished to send to her but could not for want of an oportunity. I felt to pitty him—he appears like a good hearted man. I asked him yesterday if he had an intrest in heaven. Mr. Damon proposed this, but in another form. His reply was that he thought he had known what it was to enjoy religeon since he was quite a youth—14, I think he said—but he had never made a profession. He felt as if he should if he was persistant to return home. I advised him to by all means, if he felt that he enjoyed religeon, to avale himself of the sympathy and prayrs and watchfull care of the people of God. It has been raining hard all day, evry thing appears dul and lonely. We were very glad to have Smith call tonight, for the evening has passed more pleasently. And now if I could lay my head for a short time on your arm, as I have sometimes done, and then turn over and go to sleep I should be perfectly satisfied. Whether you would or not I cannot say. Oh how anxious I am to have the time pass and have you return from that unpleasent reigeon.

* *Botomray:* bottomry, to mortgage the ship.

July Tuesday 25

Mr. and Mrs. Hunt called today. I had just left the washtub—some dresses and fine cloths that I did not like to give the woman. Mrs. Castle and her children spent the day. She appears like a very pious good lady. Mrs. Gillet has not returned from Haiwai. She makes a long tarry. I have not seen but little of the mission people since I have been here. Have recieve very little attention from them but I do not wish to complain. They know their own affairs best, and they know also that I do not attend balls and parties, neither do I wish to draw my amusement from such a source. But for all what they have done to make it pleasent for me, a stranger in a strange land, I should ere this died of enui. I wish them much happines here and hereafter.

Sunday July 30

I have been to Church today with Capt. Spencer and Mrs. Gray. He came up after me with Mr. Damon's wagon. Returned at evening the same way. Heard Mr. Damon in the morn, Mr. Hunt in the afternoon. Was very much edified both services. Wish it might be my privalage to go 2 times every Sabath, but fear I can not go once aday much longer. I find it rather to [too] fatieageing now. Am anxious to hear from you, but there has been no arivals as yet from the whaleing ground. There has been several from the States, but nothing for us. So you see we are forgotten as usual. For my part, I feel rather indifferent about it. If they do not chose to write they had not best to, but I perfectly long to see or hear from our darling Child. I hope her miniature has been a great comfort to you, for I am sure it would be to me could I be permitted to look upon it, but a greater one to look upon her sweet face. Good night, Dear, and I wish you a good night's rest.

Monday 31 July

The King* is at Kauai, so the Governer has had a levee insted. All the foreigners were invited. Had I been residing in town I would like to have gone, but it is so warm I think I have enjoyed myself best at home. Called this afternoon on Mrs. Judd for the first time. She did not call upon me untill I had been here over one or two months at least, and I felt disposed to take my own time to return it, which I have done. The Doct.'s Sister, Husband and family are stoping there at present. They came in the *Matilda*. I think they will not be much like the Judd's family but more sociall. They have not got naturalized yet, and I think they will not. While I stay we hope some to have them for near nabours, as the family who lives near is agoing to leave soon. Oh how I want to be at home—it would be dearer than ever. Yes, doubly Dear. But I desire to be patient.

*King Kamehameha III, Kauikeaouli, 1814-1854, Accession 1825.

Saturday Aug 5

The week that has just passed has been very pleasent. There has been a man-of-war here, the *Preble*. Had the Comodore on board. Mrs Penhallow gave a party on his account last Satturday eve. I did not accept any invitation or did not attend for a variety of reasons. Capt. S. and Mrs. Gray have dined with us once this week, and they have just left. They walked up this afternoon and took tea and spent the eve. I am quite well yet and think of going to church to morow if Spencer comes for me. So we are preserved from one Saturday night to another, and I desire not to forget the protecting hand that is outstreched for me, and hope and pray that you may be enjoying that same providential care and intrist in your prayrs. I crave and think I may feel assured I have.

Thursday Aug 10

I am once more alone. Mrs. Gray and I have been together since last Sabath morn. I went down to Mrs. Hoyer and went to hear Mr. Damon at the Bethel in the morning, but heard Mr. Dole*, the teacher at Punahow. He was very lengthy and I was very tired. Went back to Mrs. H., undressed and went to bed. In the evening went in to see Mrs. Young. Staied with Mr. G. untill Tuesday night. She returned with me into the vally and has remained untill this afternoon. We dined at Mrs. Damon's Tuesday with Mrs. Young. I have been helping Mrs. Gray make a very handsome evening dress. Tonight she wares it to the King's levee. She is rather dressy—goes a good deal and seems to enjoy herself, while I stay mopeing at home. I thought after she was gone you would not like me to do so and that perhaps you did not love me well enough to buy me dresses and the [word not clear] to appear as well as she does. But the thought almost made me mad, and if you are not, I will not attribute it to want of love. I have not been as well since Sunday and fear I overdone.

* *Mr. Dole:* His son founded the Dole pineapple empire in Hawaii.

Sunday Aug 13

I have not been able today to attend Curch. Mrs. Paty has been with the children and I have had a day of rest. There has two whaleships arived the past week, one of them bound home—an oportunity to send direct to New Bedford, and I have been writing some to day to send. I have not got many written, but intind to write a number. I do not feel, however, that they deserve many as they have let so many oportunitys go by unimproved. But I will not render evil for evil but do as well as I can by them. I feel that the time of my confinement is drawing nigh, and hope to be able to send the news perhaps by some of the ships that go. Was disappointed in not hearing from you, but glad to hear ships were doing so well this season. If you are as fortunate as some of the rest, think perhaps we may go home to [too] this fall. Mr. Bush has been down, but did not call on me—but no matter. I am sure of one that will not slight me when he comes, and that is your own Dear self.

Wednesday Aug 16

Mrs. Damon and Sister have spent the day here to day. Mr. D. came up and dined. He informed me of the arival of two more whale ships, one bownd home, and also an arivle across land in less than 3 months. But not one word from home, and nothing of you. Where are you, pray? All alone taking oil fast? If so, well—I if no one els, wish you succes. But what has become of Henry H.,* and all of our good friends in America? Arivals by sea and arivals across land, but not one word for us from them. It makes me feel rather bad, but perhaps it is all for the best. At all events I am perfectly willing to trust my heavenly Father for all things, both as pertaining to this life and that which is to come. Adieu.

* *Henry H.:* probably Henry Horace Terry who married Edwin's sister Thirza in 1837.

Sunday Aug 20

O Edwin, I have thought of you today a grate deal. I am not feeling well attall [at all], and do not know what I am to do or how I am to get along. After dinner today I was sick, and vomited. I asked Mrs. Paty's woman to emty [empty] the bowl for me. She told Mrs. P. if she had to emty it she would leave her. What a heart. And must I be confined without my husband or one that I can call my friend, amidst a class of people possed [possessed] of such adamantine hearts. But I will not distrust a kind providence, for I think he will raise me up friends in time of kneed. The only place that I can find consolation is at the throne of grace.

Thursday Aug 24

I have been down town today spending the day at Mrs. Hoyers. Called on Mrs. Hunt. She has just commenced housekeeping. Tried to have them take me, for I do not know what I shall do when I am sick [childbirth]. For we are destitute of any one [at] nights, even a native woman. But they declined on account of having no furniture, having disposed of it at Lahina. Mrs. Damon proposed to furnish it for me. I called there. As I came up I was feeling bad—Mrs. D. mentioned your name in connection with my expected trials, which brought tears to my eyes that I could not sappress. Mrs. Damon said if [I] would send them word, Mr. D. would fetch Mrs. Gray up in the carage. She is the only one I expect to have with me, and I do not know as I shall go untill morning. But I hope so, as I am not quite ready. I do not sleep well nights attall, and feel rather lonely. If you were here I should want you to keep awake for company. Perhaps I may not have an other oportunity to write. If not, I will here say that I love you still and do not regret comeing with you. Martha.

[Martha's child, William Henry, called "Wille" was born on the 26th of August, according to her biography. In In The Wake of Whales *the date is given as August 27th, as it is here.]*

Wednesday Sept 27

The boy is one month old to day. Mrs. Gray and I have been spending the day at Mrs. Buts, a new neighbour. She is expecting her husband evry day, full bound home. They sailed 11 days before we did. They have been very successfull. I am quite well, but feel weak yet and I fear I shall not get very strong. It is so warm and I have so little apetite at present. My apetite was extremely good at present first. The day before my babe was 4 weeks old, Mr Damon came up for me to spend the day at his house with the other ladys, Mrs. Gillet, Mrs. Gray, Mrs. Young, and Mrs. West—all sister by profession, or Brother whaleman's wives rather. I got very tired. Went and spent the night and staid untill Monday afternoon, when Mr. D. took me in the valley. Mrs. Grey was with me dureing my confinement and did for me and my child, as an own sister would have done. She staid with [me] nearly two weeks. I dressed him the day he was two weeks old, and have continued ever since without interruption. Mrs. Paty has been very kind, and I have a very good native woman who assists me about taking care of my child. Does my chamber work and my washing, for which I pay her 11 shilings a week. I could not get my washing for less than a dollar, and it would be almost imposible for one to take care of my child night and day. He is rather wakefull nights and evenings. He does not pretend sleep, but considering he is papa's only son, I suppose he must be indulged. Mrs. Gillet's Husband has arived today. The first of Oct. The Pilot just went from here and told me so. When oh when will you come, my love?

Saturday 30 of Sept

Capt. Gray and wife have call twice. They were here this after noon. I shall feel very bad when they are gone, very lonely. I have been sick all day, but have been trying to do up some dreses for the babe. Hope to feel better tomorrow.

October Tuesday 3

Mr. and Mrs. Damon called this afternoon and insisted upon my going home and spending the night with them. They are expecting several Captns. and their Leadies there to tea, but I declined with the expectation of going down town tomorrow to spend the rest of the week with Mrs Grey. Am feeling quite anxous for you to come, and cannot give you longer than untill the last of this month. I am feeling pretty well at present, rather weak.

Wednesday Oct 11

Went down as I anticipated. Returned yesterday—was somewhat fatigued. Spent one day at Mrs. Chamberlain. Went to the Mothers' meeting in the afternoon. Thursday at Mrs. Armstrong's, Friday at Mrs. Castle's. The rest of the time at Mrs. Hoyer's. Like Captain and Mrs. Gray, well shall regret much when they leave for home. There are arivals evry day, but no *Lucy Ann* yet. I am looking very anxously but Capt. McKee sais you will not be here before the 20th of next month—but I cannot think he is right. Our babe grows and improves so rapidly I wish you to come very much to love and admire him with me. Capt. G. and Lady have been up today. I with them dined at Mr. Paty's, also Judge Terril and wife. A plesant day.

Friday Oct 13

Today I have been washing and Ironing fine cloths and commenced bleaching my hat, and one for Mrs. Bates and Fanny. There has been one or two arivals today. Mr. Weider was in one of them, an English brig. Mutiny on board—the Capt, Mate and Super Cargo* Murdered. He had his wife and her servent. The brig was retaken by a youth about 19. I hope my love when you do come, there will be no trouble on board, but a full ship. Quite rainy today.

* *Super Cargo:* Officer in charge of the business of the voyage.

Oct Saturday 14

Another week has passed with its changes. Mrs. Gray went up for me this afternoon, for the purpos of my being here when they leave, which they anticipate doing on Monday. Mrs. Hoyer thinks of sending her little Daughter to the States, and thinking she will be very lonely, I have offered to spend a few days with her. We are all wishing for you to come but as yet have no tidings. With many wishes for your success and prayers for your safe return I close and retire. M.S. Brown

Monday 16

The *Jefferson* has sailed. Mary has gone, and Mrs. Hoyer is feeling very bad for she was not quite well. I went on board with them, also Mrs. McKee, and Capt. Spencer. Went outside [the harbor] and returned with the pilot. Mrs. Gray felt very bad when she left. When we left the ship, she stood waving her pockethanderchief and crying. She is a nice woman— has one of the kindest hearts a human being ever possesed. The least I can say of her is I love her like a Sister, and if I am ever permitted to meet her at home I am sure it will pleasent for both. She wished very much to see you and hear, at least to know, if we were comeing home this fall or not, but did not. My hopes however are weak, but do not dispare. Pleasent.

Thursday 19

Mrs. H. and myself have spent the day in the valley, returned very much fatieuged. Soon after our return while we were getting the children to sleep, some one raped [rapped] below. Mrs. H. went down. My ear caught the sound of your name—impatient to hear all I rushed below. Capt. Rainered had arived, and reported you with 2000, and fair prospect of being soon. It was to [too] good news I feared, to be true. I went directly to see Mrs. R., she said you would probily be here in a week. Can I realize it? I hope for the best, trusting you will make all posible haste. Another pleasent day.

Sunday 22

Just 6 months ago today since we parted. How different are my feelings today than they were on the 22 of April. Then all looked dark and gloomy. It appeared as if there was not one bright spot for me or anything to encourage me. Now all appears bright and sunshine. My Babe is well, my own health is pretty good, my husband prospects are promiseing, and I have strong hopes of meeting my beloved Ella. She has compleeted her fourth year. What a change. May I not ungratefully forget the source from whence all these blessings flow. I have left Wille this evening—asleep—with Mrs. Hoyer and been to church with Capt. Spencer. He said it would probily be the last time he would have the privalage of going with me. I hope it may be so. He has been very kind to me and Mrs. Gray, and I feel very gratefull for his attentions. I shall be rather impatient now untill you come, which I hope will be before another Sabbath. Yet I desire to wait God's time. [Signed "Martha"—then crossed out] Yesterday I spent the day at Mrs. Damons with Mrs. Gillet, just 6 months from the day I was first there and well do I remember it.

Friday 27.

Mrs. Gillet has spent the day with me. The Capt. came and dined at 4 p.m. The day passed very pleasently. I compleeted a shirt for you. Mrs. G. put a boosom* in one for her husband. And the boy was two months old. Quite a chapter of events. I hoped you would come, but no, no Edwin has arived yet. Mrs. Gillet expressed a strong wish that you might come before she left. They expect to sail next week. I anticipate going on board their ship, for they have been having a room made on deck, and perhaps my husband will be willing to indulge me with one if posible. I think it must be much pleasenter sometimes, and with a child, very convienient. Mrs. Gray had a nice cabin on deck furnished very prettily. Perhaps I shall have *next time.*

* *Bosom:* starched front section of a shirt.

Sunday 29

Another Sabath has returned and passed, but still I am alone. I had hoped you would be [here] before today. There has [been] 15 or 20 ships arived the past week, and I felt most ashured the *Lucy Ann* would have been among the number. But no, I am agane disappointed. Another week of anxiety has commenced. A little longer I must watch the avinue in vain, but hope is a sovereign balm. Were it not for that I should long ere this dispared. I am ever hopeing for some thing—eather the return of my husband, or my own return to my loved child and dear friends. And thus I suppose it will ever be, but I would not wish my hope to stop here but desire that *hope,* which is as an anchor to the soul, both sure and stedfast, entering into that within the vale. Our babe is so good, I long for you to come and see him while he is young, for it is not proper that you should lose all the infantcy of all your children. This you understand is our number, but that is altogether in the hands of God.

Monday 30.

Mr. Damon has just left. He came to invite me for the third time to meet the Captns. and their wives. Previously I have declined. Tonight I think I will accept. I wish you could make one of the company. I shall spend the night and perhaps stay longer, for I have not yet called on the Sisters that have arived within two weeks past. Mrs. Rainard and husband have called and spent some time. I am quite pleased with them on a short acquaintance. They are not however very much liked by the generality here, but we all have our friends and our enimies. Wille is not very well today. I fear he is going to have the measels, they are very previlent. Natives die dayly. It goes rather hard with them. They are so carless about exposeing themselvs. They seem regardless of consequences. One of the Chiefs here died the past week, King [word not clear], and all are sick. Not very pleasent.

Wed November 1. 1848

We have commenced another month and yet I am looking. Not yet been permitted to behold my husband for whose return I have been anxiously looking for the past two weeks. I went down on Monday eve, as I thought of doing. Spent the evening very pleasently. There was from 15 to 20 Captns. and four Ladies. Many of them very much the Gentleman. Spent two nights there, went to McKee Tuesday. Wednesday made several calls, and returned in the valley tonight with Mr. Damon. Very much fatiuge and almost sick. The babe is well and so good, I cannot describe it. Do come and see. Pleasent.

Thursday Nov 2

Today has been a most lovely day, and for want of a woman I have been obliged to wash. Perhaps you will imagin by this time that I do it all-together, but with the accomidation here for washing, I have not, nor do I feel able. I have been obliged to go to bed several times today, before I got through and did not compleet at last. The boy was very good, or I do not know how I should got as far through as I did. I dressed him about 9, and did not take him of off [off of] the bed agane but once untill sundown (bless his little life). It is a dreadfull time here to get anything done, there is so many sick, and reports says there has 14 died since yesterday morn. They have gone prepared or unprepared to meet their Judge—Solomn, Solomn thought.

Friday Nov 3

I am to [too] tired tonight to write and to much disappointed to be pleasent or social. If you had come I think you would be sory, for you would readily concluded you wife had grown cross and ugly. But I trust after a good nights rest I shall feel refreshed. Oh the Jelly and the cloths.

Saturday Nov 4. 1848

Saturday night has agane come upon us who are spaired. Enjoy it, and the comfort and consolation it would yeald me tonight to be clasped in your own arms I cannot begin to tell. My heart swells at the thought, and my eyes fill with tears. And pray what would the reality occasion? A flood of tears and a more wakefull night than the past. The natives are all sick and I have been obliged to wash and Iron all I have had done for two weeks. But I have gone beyond my streangth and feel more than half sick. Capt. and Mrs. Gillet made their farewell call in the valley today. Expect to sail on Monday. I wish, I wish, I wish you'd come.

Sunday Nov 5.

Oh Edwin, how can I longer wait your return? Day after day passes away, and night succeeds night, but I am not permitted to clasp the object of my fondest affection. It has ever been so and will it ever be so. I trust not. What if I had remained at home? How could I have endured it? I feel worse now after being with you so long. They say absence strengthens love. Be it so. I miss you more after being in your society one year than I did when I had known you but 4 months. And if Capt. Cox speaks the truth, I think it is the same with your own self. He said you talked of me all the time, and said you never was so lonely before. I am glad that I have reason to think you love me still. Perhaps you will have some doubts in regard to my love when you remember the past, but I am happy to say since I gave my heart and hand—or in other words since I became your Wife, I have been all a wife should be. And if you could see what I have seen for a few months past of other men's Wives, you would say, and that triumphantly, that you had an echonomicle wife. If I do not earn, I do not stow away chest of cloths and things for the moths. But preaching is useless practice. Will be more acceptable, so good night, for the boy is nestling and it is past 11 o'c.

Nov Tuesday 7

Near 11 oc at night. I have been spending the day across the way with Mrs. Bates, the wife of the Gentleman who took the bundle to Lahine for you. I took his place last night with my boy, but did not rest much. Tonight I am at home, alone and lonely. Oh how I want to see you. I recieved a letter for you from home last night and am answering it tonight to send by the *Thor*—it sails tomorrow or next day. The babe is not well tonight, I fear he is going to have the measels or whoping cough. I wish you were here for I want someone to lean upon—and especially nights, for you know I sleep so sound. But good night.

Wednesday morn 8

Last night my Dear I suffered in my dream what I hope I shall never realize while a resident of the S. Isle [Sandwich Island], nor for many a long year to come. No, that feeling of perfect desolation and horror I cannot discribe—I a widow and my husband's grave the deep blue sea. Language cannot express it, but the desire to return to my child and devote the remander of my days to *our* children seemed to be the most prominent. I seemed to live over in memory our past life with its varieties, and how vividly did I remember a request of yours that I should ever remain true to your memory and your love. I awoke but can not banish the thought from my mind, and as I clasped our son this morning, I felt should such an event transpire, he would be my guardian Angel and that I could put my trust in the Lord. But in the sincerity of my heart I pray God to spare us a little longer to each other, and when he sees fit to take us away, it please him to give us grace for the trial. Amen.

Nov. Friday Eve 10 1848

When last I wrote I tried to discribe a dreem. Tonight if posible, I feel worse than then. I recieved your letter today bareing date May 1 and July 25. I have dwelt much upon the subject since, and some part of your letter showed you was ferefull we might not meet agane. How can I write it? I should feel as if I had done with earth, or wish to be. But then our Dear children, who would do for them as their parents? If it is the will of

God to take you to himself, I desire to be reconciled and think I could submit. But what should I do without you? Oh, Oh, Oh I will not dwell upon it longer, but offer up a fervent petition that God will protect you and return you safe to me before many days shall have passed away . I am happy to have another proof of your love, but I knew at times you loved me. Still the past has often come up before me as you say it has with you. I have thought sometimes I would be willing to do most anything to blot out a few months of our past life. I feel a strong sensation while I write that your eye will never behold these few lines which causes my brane to grow dizzy and a faintness at my heart, and I can only exclame in an agony of spirit—"God forbid!" But in this, wise providence so order it that we may meet agane. I will now retire after endevering at the throne of grace to calm my troubled spirit. Martha

(one thought cheres me 'tis darkest just before day.)

Saturday eve 11 Nov.

Another day of anxous watching has passed, which allso makes another week. I cannot but rejoice as each week shortens the time of my anxiety, and I feel that I shall sooner know what I know not now. But I desire to be patient and willing to wait God's time, and submit to his will without a murmer. But I find my rebelious heart gains the mastery, and I feel instantly to dispare and think my cup would be the fullest and the bitterest. Oh Edwin, my Dear Husband, if you are spared to me this time, I hope you will never leave me so agane. Will you not consent to stay and share with me and our little ones what we have. Let it be more or less, for I feel this anxiety wareing upon me. For several days I have felt it wrong in me to laugh, and my love for my boy increases daily. God grant that on another Saturday night I may behold. Martha.

Drawing by Captain Edwin Brown from his logs.

[On November 11th, Captain Brown returned to his wife with a disabled ship. The following letter was written by Captain Brown to his brother Christopher, and relates what happened from the time he left Martha in Hawaii until his return.]

Ship Lucy Ann, *not far from the coast of Kamchatka, Oct. 11, 1848*

My dear brother,

    Let me thank you for two letters, one at Lahaina and one in the Ochotsh [Okhotsk] Sea. A curious place some might think for a post office, but I found it on board a floating one called the Levant *of Sag Harbor. You may judge I fared sumptuously for a while. Tis most six months since I bid farewell to my wife at Oahu, but I hope to see her in the space of thirty-five days or thereabouts. My anxiety of course has been greater on account of the delicate situation in which I have left her. Probably (in the course of human events), you have a nephew now at the S.W. Isle [Sandwich Islands—Hawaii], about six weeks old. I rejoice to hear that Theodore has a son, but don't calculate he can begin with the S.W. Islander. I have commenced this letter you see, far from any possible opportunity of sending it, but to tell you the truth, I do it for the want of other employment, for I have read all out, and the weather is too cold and disagreeable on deck for me to divert myself there. I don't think of anything that I can do at present more congenial to my feelings than to collect a few of my wandering thoughts, and transmit them on paper for the perusal of those I shall ever hold dear.*

    I have just got through cutting out a couple of duff bags ¹ *for the old cook, a six foot gentleman of the ebony race, but as good a cook as ever handled a tormenter* ². *I cut him out a couple not unlike your old-fashioned flour bags. "There," says I, "Doctor if you should ever have a family, that would make way for two such duffs as those will hold, you would always be a poor man." He showed his ivorys and says, "Yes sir, I should sir." I give them puddings three times a week, and it's really astonishing to see how quick they will demolish two almost as big as you could roll over. We have not scarcely eaten any hard bread in the cabin and there has been, near as I can calculate, ten or eleven thousand pounds of bread consumed short of fourteen months.*

Map of Captain Brown's voyage, April – November, 1848

Courtesy Charles H. Campbell & Janet T. Swanson

On the 22nd of May I got on the ground where I whaled last voyage, cruised about there a few days and saw nothing in the shape of a whale—nor of ships, and I began to feel rather down. Latter part of the month, stood in for the Kurile Isles—saw three or four ships and all concluded to go to the Ochatsk Sea, and did so on the 28th of May. I cruised about there where I had heard of whales being got, but scarce saw any, and the 10th of July I only had three whales and one a calf. At that time I had worked farther north where I had understood a ship did well the season before in the months of August and September. That being the case, I of course thought it would be no use to go there sooner than that time. Judge my surprise and deep regret when I found ships there that had been cutting them from the time I first came into the sea. Had I only known then what I do now, the Lucy Ann would without the least doubt, been brim full long before this.

By the time I got there, ships began to flock up from the Japan sea as thick as grasshoppers. Consequently, whales soon got wild and scarce, and in fact, by the last of July had deserted the grounds entirely. I started to go south, but I thought if there was plenty of whales up there last season in August and September, they must be some where, so I stuck her north again. I went up within a few miles of the Latitude 60 degrees N., the water full of ducks and all kinds of drift stuff, and no whales, so I dug out of that. The fore part of August I got back in Lat. 58, the west coast of Kamchatka plain in sight when it was clear, and to our surprise and joy, here was polar whales all around us. It was thick fog but I ventured to lower. I don't very often go myself but I was so poor and anxious I went that day and no doubt saved the whale by it. He took the second mate's line and was gone a long time, but I pulled farther than the other boats and happened to be in the right direction to catch a glimpse of him through the fog when he came up. For we could not see but a very few rods, and the old ship was far out of sight. We pulled right up to him and struck him again and again and soon turned him up.

The whale had been running about and now, "where is the ship?" was of course the next query. I got three boats towing the whale and I started in pursuit of the ship. I pulled and pulled, anxiously listening to hear the report of a gun but no cheering sound greeted my, begun to be anxious, ears; when lo and behold on my starboard beam went a big bang. "Huzzah, huzzah, huzzah boys." I slewed the boat in the direction of the report and pulled with renewed vigor. Shortly a dark speck showed itself through the thick mists, and we were alongside of the old bark again.

"Up boat, boys, how do you head then?" W. by S., Sir." "Here's a little air, boys, give her everything, loose fly gib, down main tack, keep her close to the wind there, we ought to head within a point or two of those boats, boys. Cook—grease those woods and put in two of them, ram them down solid and fire away". It was a quick response and we did fire near a keg of powder which made the Ochotsk ring. And soon we heard their well known voices a little off our lee bow, long before we could see them. Mother will say "what presumption." I should not have done it, Mother, had I not known we had a big gun and plenty of powder. This whale made us one hundred and ninety barrels.

We raised a gam of polar whales. But, says you—"What do you mean by a polar whale?" Some call them Russian whales and I suppose they are nothing more nor less than the Greenland whale, larger, and blubber much fatter. In fact, it beats anything I ever saw. A real fat one is more like sperm whale junk, almost all goes to fat. I got one that had bone thirteen and a half feet long, if I remember right.

In the month of August we took over a thousand barrels of oil. I began to think seriously of a full ship, but alas, our hopes were soon blasted. Land was astern that night, some thirty or forty miles distant. Started the try works, but gale increasing and raining. We took in the fore sail and cooled down. The weather continued much the same through the day—nothing like so heavy a gale as I have experienced, and I did not apprehend anything serious at all, and towards night, I thought there was a fair prospect of better weather.

Here I must digress a little. We had a whale in the blubber room, that being the case we, of course, had a number of casks on deck which invariably have to be taken out to make room for the blubber. Besides this, we had about fifty barrels of water and sixty of oil on deck, bone, and a good deal of the trash, consequently, we were not in the best condition to take a heavy gale. A four boat ship, you are aware, carries three boats on her larboard side, our three were to the leeward. We had been getting oil fast, and been very busy. And everything was dirty, greasy and slippery in the extreme.

The night was now closing in upon us and we were securing the last boat, chock up to the davit heads, when she fetched a sudden heavy roll and shifted all the blubber to the leeward, and hove the ship almost on her beam ends. We took in the main top sail in almost no time and started fifteen barrels of water off the leeward side as soon as possible—which together righted the ship so that she was pretty well up again. The gale now had got to be rather more severe and the sea was tremendous, in fact the ugliest I ever witnessed in all my life. They seemed to roll up in all manner of shapes and strive, which could make the most threatening appearance. Now, had it not been for the land, I should probably have wore around on the other tack, on which she would have headed the sea much better, and probably escaped any injury from them. But I chose to risk the sea in preference to going ashore. After the last mentioned work was done, I sent men into the blubber room to try and secure some of the blubber, but the ship was down so bad and there was so much grease that they could do but little good. They had not been there but a little while however, before we were eased of a burthen off our lee side without any human assistance, and in a great deal less time than man could have done it—for one of those mad cap seas seemed to fall on board of us. As they laid in the blubber room they thought the decks were coming down on them. It was a tremendous crash and the ship was completely buried up for a moment in the foam. She was soon however divested of her burden, and what a scene presented itself when she again rose from view. It was almost a clean sweep from the forward part to the after part, and I consider it very fortunate that no one was lost overboard. It happened nearly all were below, those that were on deck were aft under the round house. A little before, most of them were there procuring the boats.

About midnight, another dreadful sea struck her with tremendous force, which made her tremble like an aspen leaf. This was unlike the first sea, for that seemed to fall on board, but this struck her fair. It seemed as though it was the whole length of her, by the shock it gave me in my room. My chest was pretty well secured, and it turned over, bottom side up. The old ship presented a sad appearance on the morn. You will excuse me from attempting to give anything like a real view of this last scene, but a certain author has said that the sea, when lashed to a foam, reminds one of being on the confine of eternity.

People wonder at many things in the sea, but I wonder at the sea itself—that vast Leviathan rolled round the earth, smiling in its sleep, waked into fury, fathomless, boundless, a huge world of water drops. Whence is it, whither goes it? Is it eternity or nothing? Strange

ponderous riddle that we can neither penetrate nor grasp in our compre-
hension, ebbing and flowing like human life. Imagine a war of ten
thousand artillery with their smoke curling till every object around is
hid in its remorseless fury, and you may for some idea of the scene I
witnessed on the 14th inst.

Oahu

I arrived here and to my joy found my wife enjoying excellent
health with as pretty a little son as eyes need to look upon. A perfect
image of his father of course—blue eyes and light hair, prominent fore-
head and filled with expression. His name is William Henry for which
he received an Eagle[3] to be deposited in the Savings Bank until he is
twenty-one years of age.

The ship is going through heavy repairs. Carpenters are very
scarce at three dollars per day.

I suppose there was never so much oil taken in one season as the
last and perhaps will never be again, but whaling looks fairer for two or
three years to come, in my view, than it has for several years past.

Your affectionate brother,

E.P. Brown

---

[1] *Duff bag:* for boiling a flour pudding called "duff".

[2] *Tormenter:* tormentor, a long fork used on board ship for taking meat out of the coppers, the galley kettles.

[3] *Eagle:* former American gold coin having a face value of ten dollars.

[On December 21st, after refitting the ship, Captain Brown left Hawaii with Martha and little Wille to continue whaling. Three months later, Martha makes a final entry to her journal.]

Febuary, Thursday 8 1849

After a silence of nearly three months I agane resume the pleasent task of journalizeing. When I last laid down my pen it was with a sad and heavy heart. Immagings of future [word not clear] had depressed my spirit and filled my mind with gloom. And had it not been for a firm reliance on the promises of God, I think I should nearly have dispared. But with the riseing of another sun, how was my heart made to rejoice—my Husband was permitted to return and clasp in his arms his first born son. Proud Father, may he be long spared to you. Various have been the changes since then. After a tarry of 6 weeks at Oahu, we agane weighed anchor and sailed for the Navigators [Samoa], Opolo [Upolu], where we arrived Jan. 15. I of course, after a stay of 8 months on shore, was obliged to go through the regular process of initiating, namely sea sickness. And I had a good opportunity the first week, for we came out with a very strong wind and for a week or more it blew Tremendious. Then it was that I sayhed [sighed] for home, and then it was that Edwin turned nurse and performed all the little duties for the babe—except one. And it was really amusing to see that whaleman bathe, powder and dress that little one of four months. We remained at Opolo nearly a week. I spent two nights on shore. But was glad to get on borde the ship agane, bound still farther to the southard, hopeing soon to be there for the heat was intolerable. Since we left there we have been sailing along most of the time with a good fair wind and are now not far from New Zelland. All hands scrimshantering* pretty much. The Captain has caught the fever for a few days, and next I expect to be atacked with it. Since we left port last we have had as many pineapples, limes, Bananas, and hogs as we wanted. They are all sour now, except the latter— which by the by we are to have some part of one for dinner today. And Frank is setting the table which [words not clear] strong that the hour is approching—a warning for me in readiness [final line not legible]

* *Scrimshantering:* making scrimshaw, carving whalebone.

[From December 21st through March, the Lucy Ann *searched for and caught whales between Hawaii and New Zealand. But now the insects started to take over the ship "A log entry speaks of Martha and the steward scalding out bedbugs which shared the beds 'in quantities,' On another occasion, the Captain seriously burned his hand while trying to blow up invading cockroaches with gunpowder and 'skinned every finger on my hand, burnt my whiskers and singed my hair and shirt and what excruciating pain I was in for an hour or two.'"**

On March 28th 1849, Martha's hand appears in the Captain's log with the following entry:]

Adieu to Whale grounds and now for home and right glad am I. And now my Dear, alow me to inform you that this is the last time you are to leave, or visit these waters which to you have become familliar according to your own assertions. Martha

[On April 30 1849, after experiencing the usual gales, Captain Brown writes in his log: "Once more, bless the Lord, we are again around the Horn and riding again on the botom of my native Atlantic." On July 7th, the Lucy Ann *dropped anchor in Gardiner's Bay, returning to Greenport after 22 months at sea.]*

* *In The Wake of Whales,* p. 22

Drawing by Captain Edwin Brown from his logs.

About the Ship *LUCY ANN*

"The 309 ton ship Lucy Ann . . . had been added to the Greenport whaling fleet in 1844, having been previously registered in Wilmington Delaware. After two and a half years at sea the Lucy Ann returned to the home waters of Peconic Bay on May 1, 1847. Captain Brown delivered to the owners—Wiggins, Parsons and Cook—the very profitable cargo of 2,400 barrels of whale oil, and 24,000 pounds of whale bone. He again sailed on the Lucy Ann August 21, 1847, returning July 8, 1849 with an even greater shipment of 120 barrels of sperm oil, 2,280 barrels of whale oil and 22,000 pounds of whale bone. So great was his harvest that he had to send home an additional 20,290 pounds of whale bone by other ships.

Originally built as a merchant vessel in Bath, Maine, the Lucy Ann was first registered there on April 25, 1831. Later, after refitting as a whaler, she sailed out of Wilmington, Delaware until 1844 when the ship was sold to Greenport owners. Her final voyage out of Greenport was in 1849 and after difficulty at sea the Lucy Ann put into the port of Rio de Janeiro, Brazil, where she was condemned in 1850. However, the ship appears to have been resurrected for she was reportedly sold in 1851 in Rio de Janeiro as a whaler. Some time later the ship Lucy Ann was condemned by the British Court of Admiralty finally ending her long career."

—from *In the Wake of Whales*

Drawing by Captain Edwin Brown from his logs.

Letter from Martha to her family, telling of Wille's death.

Orient January 4, 1852

My Dear Sister and Friends,

If it is that I have yet got any friends left. If I have, why are they so silent? It is now a long time since I have heard a word from you in any form. If you knew how much I have thought of you since the death of our little Wille, I know you would think it worth your while to drop me a few lines. Here I am isolated, as it were, from all that is dear to me except my little family, and that I find has lessened very much since two weeks ago to night. Then we were all alive and well, with the exception of myself. I had a bad cold, but we all attended church through the day. Wille had on a new winter jacket that I finished of late Saturday night for evry day, but he wore it as it was new. It was blue base, just like one I had made for his father. And when he got it on, he says, "Ma, see how Illa look like Pa." Preacious child, he was permitted to ware it but three days. He appeared to be well on Monday untill towards night—he said "Ma, I sick," but kept playing. He eat but very little supper and soon asked to go to bed. He was restless through the evening. He appeared to have some feever and before I went to bed at ½ past 10 I took him up and baithed him in tepid water. He seemed to enjoy it. Put him back to bed.

He rested very well until about three, when I percieved he appeared to be hoarse. I got up and applied hen's oil freely, both inwardly and outwardly, but he breathed hard and I felt affraid he was agoing to have the croop. I could not go to sleep agane but got up with him several times. I called Mary Ann long before it was light, and had a fire made, and took him up early. He seemed to have a grate deal of feever. We doctered him with cold water through the day. His feever abated, he coughed very little, but now I feel that it was a singular cough. At night he seemed better, but we felt that his cold was tight.

In the first of the evening, Edwin went down to Mr. Holmes* and got serup of squils,* and Mr. Holmes reccommended a mustard poultice on his chest. I put on a large one. He did not have it on more than a minute before he said it pricked, and wanted me to take it off and put on a nice clean cloath on Illa, as he used to speak his name. I took it to the stove where he could not see me and put a thin piece of muslin over it and put it on agane. "There, that's nice", he says.

He sleped in the bed with us all night and we did not get up with him untill five in the morning. I gave him the squils in the evening and vomited him, but dare not leave him in the trundle bed for fear he might be very bad before I should waken, as I slept so little the night before. He was quite restless and called often for drink. At 5 I got up and gave him a large tablespoon full of castor Oil. It mooved his bowels three times through the day, and at tea time we thought him to be better. His toung looked better and he said, "Now Illa is gitting well, will Pa take Illa sleigh ride?"

He got down out of the chair about six in the evening, and walked nearly across the room to his Father and says, "Pa take Wille and By," meening to take him and rock him. He was talking with a neighbor that was in and took no notice of him. I had Martha Jane [born 1850] in my lap raidy for bed. I sat her down in the little rocking chair and took him up and rocked him. They both went to sleep immediately. Laid him into bed, went back got Martha Jane, and as I was laying her in, noticed him to throw up his arms and it seemed hard for him to breath. I put another pillow under his head, and as I did so said "I am affraid Wille has got the croop now." Mr. Conklin was just going out the door. I said, "Do come here." He and Edwin came in the bedroom with the lamp. He said he never saw anyone with it, but we all felt it was, even so.

He told what Mulford had said that day he was dooing for one of his children that he said had it, vomiting him with squils that Wille had taken several times through the day, but had vomited no phlegm.

I took him up. Edwin went over to Mrs. Young—she told him what was best to do. He went into Mrs. Pools and we workard faithfully over him. There was several came in, no one hardly knew he was sick. Mrs. Marcus Brown staid with me untill 1/2 past 10. Her husband was not well and she was agoing to give him a sweat. It stormed hard. We went down lain [Village Lane] for the Doct., but he had gone home about an hour.

We thought he could not live untill we could send to Greenport and back. We thought he was dieing at 9 oc, but he revived up agane, and agane about 10 he seemed to be going but revived agane, and asked us to rock him. We asked where it hurt him? He said it "did not hurt Wille," and I do not think he had one pain but choked to death. He had very hard strugles through the evening, but when he cried for the first half hour he hardly moved a finger, but kept calling for watter. I put nearly a pint in his mouth with a spoon. "More watter, more watter," was the last he said, and before the clock struck 11 he ceased to breath. His happy little spirit took to flight to yonder world of Joy, I trust to meet our beloved Father and Sister and many other redeemed spirets of loved friends once here on earth—and if we are permitted to recognise our friends there, may we not suppose they have already welcomed him to there little company where sorrow and pain can nomore reach them.

We could not get him to vomit after he grew worse at 6 oc. I think it was in his wind pipe. I do not [think] anything could have saved him, for I think he had enough down to have made him very sick, if it had not been so stubborn a case. While I am writing it appears like a dream, would that it were. But no, it is a stern reality. With my own hands I washed him and pined him in his winding sheet. He did not looke as if he was dead. We kept him untill Sunday from Wednesday night. Christmas eve, a sad one to us.

We have all had bad colds but are all getting better. Have not you got the letter Henry wrote the next morn after he died? Do write me a long letter, and do write hereafter once a month—pay the postage and I will do the same. 3 cents a month can not brake us. I would write Helen and Ada, but do not know where to direct to them nor Jashuay [Joshua]. He wrote us where, but I have lost the little scrap on which it was, and have forgotten. My love to all—not one execttion [exception]. I long to hear from you as I never longed to here before. Ella wished me to say that the Lady teacher had come, and she likes her very much, and she loves to go to school. She says she wants to come up there very much. All join with me in sending their love to all, and allow me still to remain your affectionate Sister and daughter,

Martha S.Brown

[the following is added at the top—two locks of hair must have been included with the letter.]

The short and darkest was cut off after he died. The other is what I cut off last sumer. This letter and hair is for all—each has a share.

P.S. agane. On last Thursday night Elibby Moore that was, presented her husband with a little daughter, a New Year's present. Isn't that smart for five months. M.

[written in the margin:]

P.S. Tell Mother now I can begin to feel some of the trials she has passed through. None but a mother can know a mother's feelings over a dying child, or when she gazes for the last time on its loved features, ear [ere] it is buried forever from her sight in the cold ground. Oh Wille, my son Wille, my heart yearns for you still, and must, I think, while life shall last. M.

* *Marvin Holmes:* proprietor of the general store, located where the Orient Country Store is now.

Syrup of squills: made from the inner scales of the white variety of Urginea Scilla. Used as an expectorant, cardiac stimulant and diuretic. Gerald Latham remembers being given this as a child. Modern remedies for the Croup (acute obstructive laryngitis) may include antibiotics, but concentrate on inhalation of steam.

Praysed be God that I have once more the oportunity of siting down with pen in hand to scrible here the events of the past week nothing in particular occured the first part of the week. we spoke an English Merchent man Tuesday the Capt sent a boat on board to get some papers he proposed to give him in hops to learn something of the war but all to no purpose he sent him a buckitt of potatoes and some pumpkings the English capt offered to return the compliment next day was of sending a little rum which the Mate very politely declined accepting. Thursday it commenced blowing pretty strong from the westward it continued to increase dureing friday and Saturday and Sunday morn it blew very hard. they were obliged to take in some sail before Seven bells it continued increasing gradualy untill noon when it blew an almost perfect gale. between one and two they close reefed the maintopsail took a reef in the foresail the only sails there was on the ship and it may with propity be said the waves were running mountain high. it is astonishing to what hight the wind will cause the water to rise in heaps I did not venture on deck all day but went several times and stood on top of the stairs in the companionway sometimes there would be a huge wave on either side of the ship another ahead and astern and the ship in a deep valley the next moment we would be mounted on the top but to be plunged agane in the depth well says the Psalmest they mount up to the Heaven. they go down agane to the depth; their souls are melted because of trouble. they real to and frow and stagger like a drunken man they are at their wits end then they cry unto the Lord in their trouble and he delivers them out of their distresses Oh that men would praise the lord always for his wonderfull works to the children of men. I felt to passes the spirit of drowning Peter. and with Childlike confidence to exclame Lord save or

$G E N E A L O G Y$

MARTHA'S FAMILY

Erastus Brewer,	(1780-1839)
m. Nancy Noble Brewer	(1783-1870)
1806	

children:

Eunice Brewer	(1807-1879)
Nancy Mariah Brewer	(1809-1893)
Joshua Bowen Brewer	(1811-1899)
m. 1840	
Harvey Brewer	(1812-1894)
m. 1839	
Edwin Brewer	(1814-1881)
m. 1837	
Samuel Noble Brewer	(1816-1860)
Helen Lovesa Brewer	(1818-1888)
Solomon Brewer	(1820-1821)
MARTHA SMITH BREWER	(1821-1911)
m. Edwin Peter Brown, 1843	
Charlotte Noble Brewer	(1823-1849)
Eliza Adeline Brewer	(1826-1888)
m. 1850	
Solomon Emerson Brewer	(1830-1890)
m. 1860	

MARTHA & EDWIN'S CHILDREN

Ella Orianna Brown	(1845-1925)
m. Charles Caswell, 1874	
William Henry (Wille)	(1848-1851)
Martha Jane Brown (Jennie)	(1850-1896)
m. Thomas Darlington, 1871	
Theodore Neville Brown	(1851-1924)
m. 1883	
William Edwin Brown	(1852-1924)
m. Elizabeth Delia Young, 1896	
Herbert Erastus Brown	(1854-1874)
Charlotte Eunicia Brown	(1856-1861)
Adelyn Isabelle Brown	(1858-1946)
(Addie) m. George Edwards, 1887	
Virginia May Brown	(1861-1929)
m. Albert R. Shaw, 1890	
Mary Lyon Brown (Minnie)	(1865-1958)
m. Edwin C. Howe, 1888	

EDWIN'S FAMILY

1st. Richard Brown, born in England
2nd. Richard Brown,
  born Salem, England 1629
  Land deed recorded in 1659, now
  "Brown's Hills," Orient. d. 1668

EDWIN'S FAMILY (continued)

3rd. Richard Brown (Ensign)
4th. Richard Brown (Captain) (1684-1748)
5th. Richard Brown
6th. Richard Brown, drowned 1770
  Widow, Zipparah Tuthill
7th. Richard Brown, m. Suzanah Young
Christopher Brown (1759-1832)
  soldier in the Revolutionary War
  m. Hannah Terry

children:

Deacon Peter Brown	(1781-1857)
m. Phoebe Rackett, 1837	

children:

Thirza Brown	(1811-1894)*
m. Henry Horace Terry	(1798-1887)
Abigail C. Brown	
m. David Tuthill, 1838	
Amanda Brown	
m. John Payne, 1839	
Mary Brown	
m. John Young, 1839	
Hannah Brown	
m. Joseph Havens, 1845	
Elizabeth (Libby) Brown	
m. William Corwin, 1848	
Christopher Brown	
m. Ruth Anna Morris, 1855	
Theodore Brown, d. 1858	
m. Hettie Hobart	
EDWIN PETER BROWN	(1813-1892)
m. Martha Smith Brewer, 1843	

*descendants of Thirza Brown—
children of William Young Terry
and Jessie Anderson Younie
who remained in Orient:

Rosemary Terry	(1908-1915)
Henry Horace Terry	(1910-)
m. Ruth Eckhardt	(1912-)
2 children	
Martha Younie Terry	(1911-)
m. Lloyd Elton Terry	(1910-)
5 children	
William Y. Terry Jr.	(1917-1986)
m. Loraine Strohmeyer	(1925-)
4 children	

THE KNOWN DESCENDANTS OF MARTHA & EDWIN'S CHILDREN

1. William E. Brown   (1852-1924)
   m. Delia Elizabeth Young
   children:
   Elizabeth Brown   (1898-1986)
   m. Alexander McNeill
   (SEE BELOW)

2. Adelyn Isabelle Brown   (1858-1946)
   m. George Edwards   (1856-1948)
   (SEE BELOW)

3. Mary Lyon (Minnie) Brown*(1865-1958)
   m. Edwin Chapin Howe   (1859-1904)
   children:
   Madeline Howe   (1892-1992)
      m. Harry Mearns, 1941
   Edwin Chapin Howe II
      m. Freda Grace Randall
      children:
      Edwin Chapin Howe III (1924-1948?)
      Nancy Randall Howe   (1927-   )
      Virginia Brown Howe   (1932-1933)
      *named after Mary Lyon (1797-1849),
      founder of Mount Holyoke College.

ADELYN ISABELLE BROWN   (1858-1946)
   m. George Lewis Edwards   (1856-1948)
   children:
   1. Mildred Edna Edwards   (1889-1975)
     m. Walter E. Prince   (1883-1918)
   2. Irma Darlington Edwards(1891-1940)
   3. Paul Kenneth Edwards   (1895-1940)
     m. Elizabeth (Sylvia) Campbell
     (1895-1974)
     2nd m. Edward Thomas

1. Mildred & Walter's children:
   Barbara Edwards Prince   (1918-   )
      m. Charles John Hughes Jr. (1918-   )
      children:
      Galen Edwards Hughes   (1943-   )
        m. Robert Zimmer
        children: Eric Zimmer   (1964-   )
      Charles John Hughes III   (1946-   )
        m. 1. Carol Stevens
        children:
        Peter Jack Hughes   (1969-1975)
        Christopher Hughes   (1972-   )
        m. 2. Debra Borthwick   (1950-   )

3. Pauls & Sylvia's children:
   Phyllis Edwards   (1919-   )
   m. Rode Miller Hale   (1913-   )
   children:
   Paul Edwards Hale   (1942-   )
      m. Adelaide Manera   (1947-   )
      children:
      Paul Bartholomew Hale   (1981-   )
      John Kenneth Hale   (1985-   )
   Roda Hale   (1946-   )
      m. David L. Gillispie Jr.   (1945-   )
      children:
      Kristin Edwards Gillispie   (1968-   )
      David Layton Gillispie III   (1971-   )

WILLIAM E. BROWN   (1852-1924)
   m. Delia Elizabeth Young   (1854-1940)
   children:
   Elizabeth Brown   (1898-1986)
     m. Alexander McNeill   (d. 1933)
     children:
     Donald A. McNeill   (1922-   )
     (SEE NEXT PAGE)
     Keith Edwin McNeill   (1925-   )
     (SEE NEXT PAGE)

Donald A. McNeill (1922-)
  m. Hilda M. Tuthill
  children:
  (twin) Donna Lou McNeill (1946-)
    m. Kenneth Waters Terry (1944-)
    children:
    Kevin Matthew Terry (1966-)
      m. Tammy-Rain Dougherty
      (1968-)
      children:
      Isaiah Waters Terry (1991-)
      Caleb Matthew Terry (1992-)
    Tracey Elizabeth Terry (1968-)
  (twin) Rosemary Eva McNeill (1946-)
    m. Kent John LeBailey (1945-)
    children:
    Nicole Rene LeBailey (1971-)
    cm. Jason Wall
    children:
      Taylor Chee Wall (1991-)
      Shelby La Ren Wall (1993-)
    Jonathan Kent LeBailey (1975-)
Kathy Jean McNeill (1954-)
  m. Patrick John Caffery (1954-)
  children:
  Meghan Elizabeth Caffery (1982-)
  Ryan Patrick Caffery (1984-)
  Kathleen Erin Caffery (1986-)
  Bridget Nicole Caffery (1989-)
  John Donovan Caffery (1992-)

Keith Edwin McNeill (1925-)
  m. Phyllis Stillman
  children:
  Laura Jane McNeill (1950-)
    m. Harry A. Davis
    children:
    Marcus McNeill Davis (1972-)
    Amity Nan Davis (1978-)
  Brenda Ann McNeill (1952-)
    m. Edward A. Evans
    children:
    Melissa Jade Evans (1983-)
    Parker Alexander Evans (1985-)

Sampler started by Martha of her family. Finished by her daughter Adelyn in 1939.
Martha's death date is an error, and should read 1911.   *Courtesy of Barbara Hughes*